INFINITY MAN

Observations of Life by an Old Soul.

Raising Your Awareness Evolving
from the Physical to the Spiritual
Along the Eternal Continuum.

Dr. Jack H. Weaver

Infinity Man
Musings and Observations of Life by an Old Soul.

Paperback (ISBN): 978-0-578-99177-1

Dedication:

To my dear wife Bonnie, my beloved children, Darcie, Hanna, and Tyson. Also to the next generation, our very special grandchildren, Tayton, Chloe, Soleil, Kaja, and Logan. May they and all the seekers who read these pages strive to find their answers and live authentic lives and come to Peace.

A Word from the Author

Following is a synopsis of portions of previous essays I have composed. This kinda sums it up for me. Man needs to "graduate" or evolve his thinking. 99% of people live their entire lives in the physical sense. They are into their egos in that they believe their physical being is really all they have, all they are. They fail to go deep within to realize or become aware that the physical is so very temporary. The only thing that is lasting is the spirit. It is energy and energy cannot ever be destroyed.

By coming to the realization that our lives are just temporarily leased to us, we do not own them, for they disappear and our essence, our real permanance exists only in our spirits, our souls. At our arrival, we are assigned a name and we assume an identity. When you start to really learn to acknowledge this fact, you gradually release yourself from ego-centric desires. You begin to really see for the first time. You are not as attached to possessions, nor do you need them for " security" per se. You do not desire all the trappings of a fake and materialistic life. Less becomes more and less is enough. You recognize the connections with all living things and see that they are just briefly visiting too. You become more empathic and understanding of the travails of others. You want to be of service and live a life of meaning and live it with love. You come to learn that it is not a competition for we are all in this together.

You do not judge. You do not need to "win" in that your gain is at the expense of another's losing. The thing is, once you truly know and feel and accept the temporary nature of everything around you, you surrender and you gain faith. You know we are all connected and ONE with all that was, is, and will be, forever into eternity. You become more appreciative and serene in your daily activities. You know that to "die' is to merely move on to your next assignment, directed by the Devine. Everything starts to make more sense in that you see the perfection in the entire system.

I was blessed to observe the physical death of the 3 year old daughter of a very dear friend. Her organs were shutting down due to spina bifida. I was 31 years old. I was with her on a hospital gurney with a nurse. Her parents knew she was dying and did not want to be there at that moment. I did. She was dressed only in panties. Her body was totally bare of clothes or a sheet. I was looking down at her and suddenly I witnessed and felt this energy. Her left big toe was slightly beyond her other foot in length. Instantly I saw and heard this "whoosh". A white vapor shot up from the tip of her left big toe and enveloped her entire body in a mini-flash. It shot up from the top of her head and exited at the apex of the room, where the walls and ceiling met at the farthest corner. It was clearly pure energy. It was her young, innocent and pure unspoiled spirit leaving a body that was defective and she was now free. I instantly witnessed salt crystals form a crust in the canthus and corners of both eyes. What was two moist eyes before was now salt. And I witnessed pure and Devine peace in that very moment. I had just been chosen to witness her ascension and I was spellbound by the beauty and wonder of it all ! It was so obvious that her spirit had departed and there was just a shell left behind. That defective and seriously flawed body was of no use anymore to her for she was released from it. It was such a beautiful and assuring event to witness. If I had blinked I would have missed it. I asked the attending nurse if she saw anything and she said she had not. She missed it. I was blessed. I felt the correctness and order and beauty of her passage. This precious young being was liberated! It was a most awesome experience!

To live in your spiritual essence is to live in a bit of heaven while on earth. Obviously, heaven is a state of lasting Nirvana whereas here is merely our proving ground, our test. Here we strive to arrive to that state where things just do not affect you in the same way as when you break away from the temporary physical and live in the enlightenment of the spiritual realm. It takes time and acute observation and deep introspection to reach this awareness. Of course we can never completely arrive to this place. But the seeking is part of our earthly journey and that striving is its own reward. Once you truly accept that you shall discard your physical body soon enough, you will be OK and accepting of what mysteries and new adventures lie ahead.

The more actualized you become the higher your energy vibrations become. Thus, when you proceed onward to the next level, your higher frequency propels you to a more advanced incarnation in some form in some place. There, you do more work and thus move forward through eternity. The spirit is where all things that matter and last truly reside. So, our challenge becomes to get to know and feel this truism in this brief and temporary physical presence and go within and live in the spirit world more permanently as you are also of this physical world. If you suffer great losses but you have discovered how to reside in your spirit world, you will have everything you shall ever need. All will always be OK. The journey is the reward.

So again, learn to devote your energies to developing and experiencing life's experiences at the spirit level. The rewards are permanent and everlasting thruout all eternity. Everything will start to make perfect sense to you and you will just know that all is as it is meant to be, and it is OK. ...Be at Peace...

Table of Contents

ESSAY 1:
What is Life??

Life is so many things. The single most relevant definition of LIFE, to me, is OPPORTUNITY!! Opportunity to live a human life. To learn, experience, savor, try, succeed, experiment, test, fail, suffer, choose, endure. To love, be loved, commit, feel, accept, deny, compete, think, join. So many more wonderful things!

Oh my God, what a Divine gift is given to each single human being on this planet called Earth! Other words come to mind for what life is, for it is everything. It is truly a gift from God. It is a huge test also. It is never-ending, for it is but a part of a continuum for all eternity. Thus, it is never over. It may change form. Actually, I am certain it does. It is hard, in different ways, for each single person who ever lives.

It is not a very long visit we have in this present shape and form we occupy so temporarily. Do we pay attention in our singular life? Most really do not. Most live in fear and uncertainty. Most do not ask many questions and thus, simply meander through life with no real answers. Pinballs with no compass or real destination in mind. Randomness. One must be willing to explore and take risks. These risks are not meant necessarily to be dangerous to achieve an Adrenaline high, for that seeking can also serve as an escape, a numbing of sorts. The risk for truly seeking humans is to venture deep within oneself and ask the toughest possible questions.

Who am I, really? What principles do I live for? What do I value and why? What is truly most important to me? What meaning does my life have to me? What is my meaning for all humanity? Does meaning really exist or matter? (It does) What purpose do I have? Do I live with passion? Why not? What is missing? Am I strong enough and mature enough to face every single challenge before me and am I brave enough to use all my will, effort, and resources to overcome this current, and temporary obstacle? Will I become wise enough and secure enough within myself, to realize that all tests are temporary? Even a life-ending illness is temporary. How will I face this and conquer it also?

Will I be capable of going deep enough inside myself to know that no matter what events happen in my life, I will learn valuable lessons from each and every single one, IF I am truly paying attention! Will I be wise enough and have such strong conviction that God placed me, specifically me, in this place in this form at this time for a reason? That reason is known by God and my task is to discover MY reason for being here in this essence. For when I discover MY reason, it will be God's reason also, for he tasked ME with this current and specific "assignment". Thus, I know to the depths of my soul that all will be as it is meant to be for ME.

God loves me unconditionally and I trust in HIM totally and forever! He made me who I am. We are all made in His image, as we are taught and I do believe this. I honor this and do not complain or question. I accept these concepts with total and absolute confidence. Of course, I take all the time necessary for me to ponder. Even on my deathbed, no matter if it be a short or long life, I will thank God for my life. My faith and convictions are bedrock strong!

I have such peace and acceptance in my life in that I have done my work and continue to do so, for I just KNOW! I know my purpose and I know totally who I am, as best as anybody can, I do believe. I speak not from arrogance, far from it. In fact, I feel humbled by most everything. It is just all so perfect, even the perceived flaws and imperfections are perfect. I am in a place of peace and in comfort with the "security" that peace provides for me.

WOW! What a marvelous experience life is! It is truly a wonder! I am in total and absolute awe! No person, event, boss, spouse, child, government, parent, or circumstance will ever alter my perception of who I am at my core! I am so blessed to know ME and know my God is my God, period! This feeling and connection has zero to do with religion and everything to do with spiritual connection to the Divine! I do know with all my heart and soul that everything in the universe is connected. As stated so many times in my essays, we are NOT separate, we are ALL connected, as ONE! So obvious!

Thus, people and their choices do not bother me. Even when they affect my life, they do not affect me personally. For I know my truth and my reality and no external happenings will ever supersede my internal, to my core, Divine compass. I see things very clearly. Even when I make an error, which I do often, I try to examine it and learn from it. So the error is not "wrong" per se. Rather, it is a teaching moment and yet another opportunity for growth. This is a gift, not a failure.

It is interesting to me as I compose this and other essays. How many people have a clue as to what I am talking about? Not too many, I would sadly venture. What I find intriguing is that I do not care much at all, as to whether they dismiss me as a "looney bird" or not! This is not about "them", per se. This is about me, (and other seekers), my and our journeys-within, the questions, the processing and the answers. I have no attachment to what others think of my "meanderings". What others believe is external to me, and my answers, as are everybody's, I do believe of necessity, are internal answers.

I would have some hope that more people follow a similar path. A self-examination that leads one to meaning and purpose in one's life. Without such a journey inward, true peace and contentment will never be found. That life lived unexamined at the deepest level is a lost opportunity that will result in waste of the most precious gift in the universe. A tragic and sad result and ending, I would state with true conviction.

ESSAY 2:
Whose life is it, really? Is it "My" Life?

I have wondered and do ponder, at times in my life, if this is really "my" life? When I have attempted to live as consciously as I have, and made decisions based on all the information and everything I could gather at that time, and ended up wherever, what "control" did I really have? I am here, now, in this situation with this life at this time. It just seems like such happenstance at times, due to factors we do not consciously plan. So, I am concluding that this life my mind and body is now experiencing is not actually a life "owned" by me, per se.

Yes, I am the present form of this life, but God created this life for me and all the circumstances this life has experienced and shall continue to experience. Thus, there is no "me" per se. There is this life form that is really God's life ie. energy, in my physical form at this time. So, no ego needs to exist when I recognize this deduced fact. It is God's life and He directs everything so as to allow me to continue to grow and develop, if one chooses to try to do so. I do choose this.

I have no beginning and no end for I am One, with God. This concept is not my opinion. It is not just something I believe. Rather, it is something I know, I feel! I am ONE! We are all One but too few realize this. They are just not aware. My essense is what God placed me in at this time. These are my circumstances. He is interested in my performance within these circumstances.

So, knowing this is not really "me", but Him, I can release resentments, regrets, anger, frustrations, disappointments, etc. for I do know on some level, that what is, is. It is all so temporary, transitory, and brief. I really do trust! How can I not and still retain my core faith and beliefs in His Divine guidance and wisdom? Thus, I am confident in being His follower. God is the original and ultimate GPS. I follow Him with curiosity, admiration, wonderment, and with confidence it will be always be OK. I surrender my life to Him for it has always been His life and I am wise enough and blessed enough to recognize and embrace this fact. I am merely "leasing" this life. It is His, not mine to "own". It is so fundamental for me to feel this at my core.

It is so true to me, as is the fact and trust the sun always comes up in the East, and each day we are born anew to wonder and appreciation and gratitude. Life is just a miraculous event and to continue to marvel at it every single day makes me aware how superbly spectacular everything really is in this endless quantum universe! I mean, WOW!! It is just all so way beyond perfect! Really, how utterly cool is that!? How brilliant to have put this all together and we humans are just so totally primitive, a mere sub-particle of a speck of dust in the entirety of creation of the universal, endless heavens in the divine celestial soup.

NOTE....When I say I surrender my life to Him, I am referring to the innate knowledge and supreme confidence I have that I am One with Him, as are we all. I am Him and He is me. All the same universal energy. No demarcations or boundaries exist. We are all "pieces of God" so to speak, but much deeper than that. So, my service or surrender is not to try to "convert" others to my way of thinking. When humans speak of converting, it is customarily to a specific religion or school of thought. Thus, I am right and you are not, the type of thinking that is so divisive. To recognize, at one's bedrock core, that we truly are all

ONE with God, in that God is within each one of us, all of us, is the polar opposite of divisive. The fact I am acutely aware of this so deeply strengthens me on a daily basis.

I am saddened and disappointed that so few seem to even barely understand or care to try to comprehend any of this. Where are the true searchers? They are out there. I am certain of this. How many, I do not know. I do not feel much optimism when I observe the human condition today. We are going backwards as a civilization and the human race "experiment" is doing very poorly. The arrow is pointing down much more than up. In fact, I see very few ups at all. "Progress" and more sophisticated "things" are only up in the minds and values of very naive and ignorant individuals and nations. Tick, tick, tick....

ESSAY 3:
God, Jesus, Fear

I refuse to believe that God wants you to follow Him by using fear as an incentive. Fear of consequences is not a tactic of love. It is intimidation and it does not generate love. I believe God wants us to follow Him out of respect, love, and trust. I believe the concept of fearing God was cultivated by the church to serve the church, not to serve God. You obey the church, ie. God, or else!

Also, primitive people fear what they do not understand or comprehend. Man has been able to use this fear as a means of control, and by tying it to the church and God, it is a very effective way to manipulate people and their thinking, even today. As for Jesus being God, in a sense He is, but really, Jesus was God incarnated as a man so people could relate to a human figure, like themselves. Thus, they could better hear God's message. On the cross, Jesus cried out to his Father, why have you forsaken me? God reassured him, as a spiritual being, that he would have everlasting life. As we all can also have. We are all children of God, just as Jesus was. So to pray to Jesus as if Jesus is God is not necessarily accurate to my thinking. Remember, Jesus lived among his fellow human beings for 30 years before he began his 3 year ministry. His mission was to spread the word of God, his Father, and our father too! So, rightly or wrongly, (Is there a right or wrong here, I think not), I choose to connect to God directly, rather than via His son.

Also, all these terrible things that have happened in the human experience for eons and continue today, are not the work of God.

They are totally and solely the results of free choice that God granted human beings. This is a grand experiment for us, devised by God, but God knows how it will end. We are just jumping thru the hoops as a weeding-out process to give us an opportunity to receive God's message or not. Again, free choice! As individuals, one can choose to get the message or not, but as a human race, I feel our fate is sealed.

Humans are responsible for all the misery in the world. And it will never change because it is wired into the entire animal kingdom, man included. All species destroy those who are different, not like them. Deer destroy the injured and weak or different. Chickens peck to death the runt. "Half-breeds" are ostracized or attacked. Animals and humans want everyone to be like them. This is a fact of life. Destroy those who do not look, act, behave or think like you do. Kill those whom you do not understand.

As the world gets smaller and more people fight over the diminishing resources, land, water, food, jobs, housing, etc, wars will always be with us until we destroy each other and the world in the process. Man will eliminate itself and destroy most all life because it can and there is no reason to expect co-operation. The strong will always seek to dominate the weak even if they destroy everything in the process. If they can't have it all, nobody will have it. What an evolved way to think! That is love?!

The end is getting ever closer because the "toys" now available to mankind and nations are capable of total annihilation of all life as we know it. Pessimistic, sadly so of course, but that is the reality that I am witnessing. I just see no positive trends to change things, with human beings as they are. The human race has a serious and fatal flaw and it will prove to be its own undoing. When one looks from a vantage point high above, this is so apparent to me. It is what it is.

ESSAY 4:
Cosmic Consciousness

I believe there is a consciousness and order to everything. People ask, "What is the point"? I believe there is a point and that is to raise one's awareness, development, spirit, et al. to an increased plane, a level higher than what you were born with. One's consciousness is raised and how much it is raised is up to each individual to ascertain, endure, discover, explore, test, examine, suffer, and ultimately learn and grow from. We should strive to achieve a higher vibrational frequency in the lifetime we are presently living.

We are all born to certain circumstances, in different places and times, with our own individual parents with unique DNA specific to us alone. We are tested our entire lives by all sorts of unforeseen events and circumstances. Many are out of our control, many are self-induced. How we make our adjustments, what we learn, what we overcome, achieve, etc. is mostly in our hands. What is not in our hands we adapt to and move forward as best we can.

I believe we must always seek our truth, not society's truth or approval. Our truth is inherent in who we really are, what vibrational level we are on and that truth is God's truth as He is the cosmic entity who gave us life. Thus, He gave us our truth and one challenge we have as human beings is to identify and to live our God given truth as much as humanly possible. I also believe as long as you know the truth in your soul you may, being human, sometimes stray or deviate due to circumstances at hand. But, as long as your truth in your heart is never surrendered, you are pure and will continue to vibrate at a higher level.

I think one test we are given is to try to surpass the vibrational level of our parentage and past and present genealogy. To accomplish that is proof you are elevating beyond from whence you came and that is all one should hope for. It is a barometer that you and your life has transcended in your single lifetime. I believe all "bad" things that happen to us and to loved ones contain a message and a learning and must be looked upon from a much higher plane, looking down from above, so to speak.

We must detach and be quiet and pray and be patient. There was a purpose for this event happening. We may never come to make sense of it but when we ourselves leave this earth, the truth will be revealed and we will have our peace and understanding. Our task is to trust, to trust in God's wisdom and to be patient. Know it is always as it is supposed to be.

We can question, blame, curse but true growth and peace can only come with acceptance of what God has in mind for us and for the human race. Remember, nothing is permanent. Everything is constantly changing all through the many universes and man is no different. Life exists in so many places and in so many forms, why would it not be perfectly natural for man to destroy himself and life as we know it? I am certain that higher, more evolved life forms exist and will be revealed in other far off galaxies. I have zero doubt that man is so very primitive and so low on the evolutionary scale that we are beneath amoebas in the grand scheme of things.

Just look at what we have done and are doing to the planet and to ourselves. How can we be called "intelligent life" when we destroy much more than we create? We hate more than we love? This is a very undesirable species that will weed itself out from existence in the cosmic soup. It will be weeded out because it is not a constructive species. Higher, more developed life forms will survive and thrive as we disappear. That is what evolution is all about. We, being inferior, die off and other entities thrive because they are more advanced and they do not destroy; they create, love, accept, help, grow, develop and improve.

ESSAY 5:
Insecurity

I believe a very significant portion of American society consists of people who are, at the core, very insecure. They tend to seek "security" in all the wrong places. They are very materialistic and think the more "things" they possess, or appear to possess, elevates them in the eyes of others. Thus, they perceive themselves to have "value, respect, even love".

When all is stripped away, the bottom line is everyone wants and desires to have love and value and worth to others. They want acceptance and validation of who they are, by other human beings. Thus is born the need by too many to try to get these needs met by external and destructive means. The more things, money, power one has the more I will like myself and the better person I am and the more people will love, respect, notice, fear, etc., acknowledge my presence and importance. Thus, I am somebody and I matter. That is the fact of all of it.

Rather, it is better to accept at your core, that you are created by God, as is everything in the universe, and thus, you inherently have value, as does everything in creation. This lack of belief that our society perpetuates is that one must do all these actions driven by motives that are for the sole reason to fill that huge void most seem to have in their souls. We want "security", answers, etc. yet fail to recognize that are not obtainable from any of these outside methodologies.

All our answers to all our questions are right there within us all the time. We just do not take the time or make the effort to look within. We scramble and scurry thru life always wanting. We want so many things but we only need one thing. We only need to rediscover that we are the source of our own security and that security comes only, only, only, from accepting ourselves, loving ourselves, being secure within ourselves!

This can only come by looking around us and marveling at and truly appreciating all this marvelous creation and that we are but a tiny part of. Our security comes from within. Our love comes from within. When we accept God's plan for each of us, He will guide us to where we are potentially able to go, as long as we take the time to be patient and observe and do our share by putting forth the effort to truly actualize His plan for us.

In our society, we have placed our values in all the wrong places. We anesthetize ourselves with drugs, alcohol, work, sex, toys, games, food, cigarettes, etc. etc. We dominate others, we induce fear to control others, we bully, we intimidate, we label and judge others, we seek to destroy those who are "different". We fail to see the necessity, gifts, and beauty of diversity. We essentially are failures as human beings and as a society, in my observations and opinion. We just must be right and you must be wrong, thus, I should and shall attempt to destroy you. You are less and I am more and I will prove it!

Again, this all comes from a strong sense of insecurity, as people and as a society. It seems to have always been so and it is getting much more dangerous and much worse. I am not at all optimistic for the human race. So, I conclude, to be able to cope with all this madness, one must just be responsible for oneself and our loved ones as best we can, and try to enlighten those who are willing and capable of listening. Hopefully, this is family and those we love and care deeply about.

It is interesting to me to just try to keep my own ship afloat and observe the behaviors of all those around me. It bemuses me somewhat as I watch the dance of the moth before the flame. For I can foresee the outcome and there is absolutely nothing that can be done on my part. It is their dance and they must do all the steps. I can only observe and form my conclusions.

ESSAY 6:
Human Beings, the Flaw

Human beings are very flawed in their composition. The flaw is not with the design of the human body, but in the free choice that we have to act as we wish to act. Personally, I do not observe hardly any progress in all the millions of years in how we behave toward one another. We take, we destroy, we conquer, we hate, we envy, we dominate, etc, etc. The problem is that our technology has grown much more destructive in such a way that it will destroy us before we are able to evolve beyond all these primitive needs and wants.

We will use this technology to destroy life as we know it. I have concluded, via observations of behaviors over the millennia, that humans do not change their behaviors enough to be able to reverse or alter the final outcome. We are destroying this planet and we will destroy ourselves in the process. The planet will adapt and survive after man has eliminated himself.

This planet will self-correct as it returns to balance, which is the way the entire universe operates, i.e. equilibrium, balance, order, all principles necessary for a forever universe. And the principles that man does not observe because he chooses to ignore them, will discard him. Thus, man will eliminate himself from the equation soon enough. The system shall always survive and the entity out of synch with the system never does, cannot and will not survive. That is not the way of a balanced and orderly system. Man is disruptive to the order of every system he is evolved in. That is just the nature of man, thus, in my opinion, it is just a matter of time before the system corrects and eliminates the source of the disorder. Man will do this all by himself. The system will just keep on seeking and maintaining its equilibrium.

This is so evident in these times. Because of the actions of man, the planet is already fighting back, more fiercely than ever. All these things that man is doing to our home have a cost and a consequence. Man is fighting against everything and each other, just like they have always done. We are on the cusp of the end point or at the minimum, a point of no return. No return to the simple ways of days long ago. Except the days long ago were just like the days today, for man is not capable of learning anything or evolving beyond his own self-interests.

So, we have reached, or in many ways surpassed the tipping point. Too little, too late. However, these coming changes are necessary. For order is necessary. I can accept this fact. I am seeing all of this as a huge cosmic experiment and game, of sorts. It is just part of the plan, something I have total trust and belief in. Actually I do not believe it is an experiment at all; it is as it is supposed to be. So be it...

ESSAY 7:
A Life of Meaning

A life of meaning with purpose and service given to others is a preferred life vs. just seeking "happiness" for oneself as the primary goal for being alive. How can one be truly happy or satisfied if your life has no real meaning?. Most people who choose to die by suicide do so because they do not perceive their life to really matter to anyone else and thus it no longer matters to them. Not being "happy" is not the lead cause or reason for ending one's life.

People can unconsciously slowly commit suicide in many ways. They can abuse and neglect themselves and just wait it out towards the end and then may ask themselves, "Is this all there is? What was the point?" And for them, there was no real point, so why not just wither away? Who cares? Studies have revealed that most people who consider themselves "happy" mainly serve themselves and put their needs first. Thus, they are mostly takers, rather than givers. The givers may not be perceived as truly "happy" and I believe this could be true because how can one be truly happy when so many others are wanting and in dire straights? The givers can see their limits and the takers could care less. Not their problem, they state.

Who dictates that being happy is the most admirable goal? The pursuit of happiness does not mean it will be achieved. Personally, I believe happiness is a state of being that can only be achieved from within. And it most certainly cannot ever be attained via wealth, power or materialistically. I also believe it can only occur in periods of time, not in a sustained state. And why would be sustained happiness be something to be desired or even expected? How can growth, empathy, stimulation, contribution evolve from such an unnatural state?

Life is meant to be lived fully engaged and to live an evolved life requires many things. Among those things are challenges, hardships, suffering, learnings, risks taken, fears faced and conquered, hard work, accomplishments, goal setting and achievements, continual growth, giving of self, teaching others, setting an example, et. al. All these things ebb and flow and some periods of happiness are hopefully included along the way. But total happiness all the time as the ultimate goal? Just not possible or realistic.

I also believe that being of service, in some capacity, in the enhancement of the quality of life of others, is the only way to reach some degree of lasting happiness. The happiness and satisfaction that comes from the knowledge that your life does matter to others and has mattered. You have grown your life through personal sacrifice and effort beyond what many are willing to do. Thus, you have truly earned the happiness that you have. No other person, event, or thing will provide you with lasting happiness. It is totally up to how you live your life, and again, it arises from within. That kind of feeling can never be taken away by circumstance or the efforts of others. It is who you have become, who you are, what you stand for. You are ONE.

Therefore, you are as happy as a person can hope to be, for you have done the work! So when you close your eyes for the final time you can justifiably allow yourself a satisfied grin for you have done your very best and you have appreciated and attempted to have made the most of all the gifts God has given you. Look forward to the next adventure with gratitude, anticipation and excitement, with God's blessings, for you have tried to be true to yourself and been of service. I think God kinda likes that.

ESSAY 8:

Masks...Our "need" for them vs. Spiritual Liberation

How do we develop masks and why? As infants, we have a primal need for love and security. To get those needs met, we learn soon enough that to behave in certain ways, and thus to address the sources of these essentials for our survival, we develop behavior patterns. We learn to please our parents, and others, to get what we want. If I behave in this way and do not do that, then I gain approval and rewards.

As one gets a little older, one realizes that they may have other desires that, if openly expressed, perhaps may jeopardize their "standing" or "image" as presented to others. One risks disapproval. So, you learn to start hiding or not revealing certain things to others. Everyone needs love and approval. We all want to "fit" in. We want to be "normal" or at least appear to be to others. But what happens as we begin to form our own identities and start living our lives? We get into internal conflicts. What is "safe" to reveal or share? And to whom?

Young children are their true authentic selves. They are totally honest and unfiltered in what they want and need. They are not yet "programmed" as to what is "expected" of them by family and society. But growing up becomes more complicated. When we try smoking, we do so in secret. We do not want our parents to know. We are experimenting, trying out new and risky behaviors, rebelling. We are forming our own opinions and making our own choices, just to please us, not "them". But we are also paying a bit of a price too. We feel some guilt and shame because we feel we are doing something forbidden, something "wrong". Something that we must hide from our parents. We do not want to disappoint them. So we are learning that to deceive is something required to get our real needs met.

In school, we have a genuine need to be like everybody else. We want to be part of the "in crowd". We learn to conform. In doing so, we can often find ourselves in turmoil. We sometimes say and do things we do not really mean, down deep. But we yield to the masses. If we have bad grades, we lie about it to our parents. We want to protect ourselves and shield them. We help spread rumors and we know that is not a good thing to do. If one has gay feelings or gender conflicts, we deny them and suppress them. We become someone who we know we are not. We feel we must do this, just to survive.

We may go to college or trade school and sometimes study what our parents wanted us to study. We may hate it. We flunk out, on purpose, to escape. We get a job because we must earn a living. We have no respect for our stupid overpaid boss and we grow to hate our needing to stick it out there. We may start to drink or have affairs or get into drugs, just to escape our situations. What is actually happening is we start to resent our own lives. We have become so far removed from our authentic selves. So far distanced from whom we wanted to be or feel we could have been, "if only". We may blame others for our dire circumstances. All these years we have worn a mask as to who we really are just to "fit in" in this modern world.

It is only by recognizing this fact that we start to really grow in the only way that is sustainable. We must learn to get in touch with our deepest feelings, our souls, and begin to gain control of our real authentic selves and hopefully regain our lives. We must dig deep within and start identifying who we really are. When a gay person who has lived their secret all their life finally realizes that their self-induced denial, "shame and guilt" is slowly destroying them, can they gain the tools to save themselves? They are living a lie, for the sake and approval of others, while they are dying inside. Those that do finally come out, after decades of deceit, show supreme courage in doing so. But they come to realize they must finally do this to survive. They must discard their mask and go naked before the world. Those who can do this finally feel such relief, such peace, such connection, finally, to who they are. What a risk, what a quantum leap they have taken!

Who among us would choose to be born with very unattractive features, gay feelings, or gender conflicted, or disfigured, or 5 foot 2 inches as a male, or 6 foot 10 inches as a female? Who would want to be born with a cleft palate, spina bifida, blind, etc, etc? Everybody wants to be "normal ". Life is difficult enough, who would willingly want additional burdens? We wear our masks to protect ourselves but these masks are not protecting us at all. Seekers come to recognize this fact. God gifted us our life. We, as spiritual beings, must strive to be accepting of this precious gift.

There is absolutely no way a person can live a non-authentic life, one that denies the feelings one did not ask for from God, and be honoring God! He grants us life, but there are conditions. He tests us. Why? Because He wants to challenge you to become all you can become. You cannot reach anywhere near your full potential if you deny the feelings that God gave to you at birth. It is not possible to live a spiritual life, as God intended, if you deny God. For if you deny who you are, you are denying God for it is He who gave you these deep feelings you have. And we ALL know our deepest wishes and feelings. They are who we are!

For most, it just never happens. It is too hard. It is too dangerous. For some, it can take a lifetime before one can face the truth of his/her life. It is very, very difficult to be authentic. People know you as one identity. To learn that person is not who they perceived them to be, can be very threatening to all involved. I do not believe it is necessary to announce to the world, but it is required to know who you are to yourself, and to not feel any more shame or guilt. To be real to yourself and to others is to gain your own respect and the respect of others who truly admire your honesty and courage to take that huge risk to finally remove that mask you have been wearing your entire life.

If you lose some family or friends, that is their loss, not yours. You have gained much more than you have lost, for you will have reclaimed yourself and that is priceless. You will be meeting your Maker, naked, pure and real, and that will very likely please God. He knows you did not question Him. You finally accepted yourself and in doing so, you have accepted Him and you shall reap your just reward. You shall have your well deserved peace on Earth as it is in Heaven.

ESSAY 9:
The Box

Ah yes, the box! What is the box? It is so many things! As a child the box is that secure place that our parents provide for us that is safe, secure, and full of love. We are fed there, cared for there, caressed there. All our needs are met there. It is the place to be. As we get a little older, we start to push against the sides of that box. We note that it is becoming a bit uncomfortable there. We perceive there are things outside that box that we want to check out.

So, we eventually venture out of it. We explore. We get into some trouble. We make some "mistakes". We can endanger ourselves. We can possibly bring harm. There are consequences. We get punished. We are put back into that box and when we venture out, things happen. So we start to learn that to go out of that box can be a risky thing. The box starts as a crib, then a playpen. It then morphs into a room, then a house. Then the yard, school, neighborhood, town, county, state, country, world.

So, soon enough, we go to school. We have escaped partially, for a few hours, that home box. But alas, there is now also a new box at school! A new set of rules with consequences. You obey the rules, stay in the school box, and all is good. You dare to dribble out, break a rule, there are once again, consequences.

You learn thru programming, that to ever dare leave the box that is provided "for you" is to have a consequence. A price will be paid.

It is very inconvenient, sometimes even dangerous, to challenge the borders of the box that work, society, and government imposes upon its "citizens". Obey this law, think this way, accept this "fact", do the job in this manner, pay this tax, follow this "leader", obey this boss, do not ask questions, trust this action, do this and don't do that, etc. etc.

So the question, and challenge, becomes for each of us, do we choose the easy, convenient, comfortable path and never take the risk that stepping out of that box entails? If we fail to take this risk at the appropriate times, do we feel we are growing, in character, intellect, spirituality, and morality? If we choose to stay in that box, as so many do, so be it. The vast majority of people are pure followers. It is too stretching and requires too much effort to challenge the system and the powers that be. They just settle and adjust their comfort zone for it is so much easier. Their mantra becomes, Whatever, it could be worse.

In my observations, the vast majority of people simply do not give a damn. They just take whatever comes their way and figure out the best and simplest way to live a settled, comfortable, easy life. No real effort is expended. No true goals, just drift and land where they land. Make the most of it. No core beliefs of true integrity to God's plan. No striving to try to reach that potential that is within all of us. Not my problem, they say.

Having made this statement, of course many exceptions exist. But for the vast majority, this is the reality. They are "comfortable enough" in their box. And society rewards you and government celebrates you by tossing you a few crumbs from time to time so you stay "content enough". Gotta keep that box just comfortable enough so you do not dare venture out! Or else!

ESSAY 10:
Reframing Events, Towards a Positive Outcome

On the radio today, they were talking about an explorer, Earnest Shackleton, who was warned not to try to get thru Antarctica because the ice was too thick that year in the early 1900's. He went anyway and the group all got stuck. After almost a year, they finally all returned home safe. The thing is the leader knew he had made a horrible mistake, yet he was able to put it behind him and tackled the problem head on and came out better in the end. He faced that adversity and confronted it without looking back. OK, I made a horrific miscalculation that may kill us all, so what am I going to do about it?

I perceive myself, rightly or wrongly, to be a bit different than many people in lots of ways. I realize I most likely have enough severe blind spots in some areas but I do believe I have some gifts and very clear vision, to me, that I feel very blessed to be aware of in this lifetime. I am who I am and I have taken some risks and I have made some mistakes. Such is life in the arena. Nobody or no employer or government entity has taken care of me and thus, in my opinion, left me handicapped and puffed up by being untested, yet believing I was omnipotent. Allow me to just let it go and get over it and move onward, always onward!

Over the last 6 years, my wife Bonnie and I have maintained 3 residences and traveled extensively. It eventually proved to be too exhausting and harried. It was very expensive also and we had to get out of it and slow down. We have now rid ourselves of all the maintenance of "places" and traveling headaches. Thus, we have "done that" and are now aligning ourselves to another new adventure, one of simplicity. We have rid ourselves of many unnecessary burdens. In doing so, we have gained more control over our lives.

We have satisfied the travel bug these last 25 years and made life-long friends and memories in the process. Priceless and comforting reminiscences in our coming golden years. Very satisfying years well lived. We just want simple now. Centered in VT where life is easy and not complicated. We control the pace. It is a nice fit for us. No social pressure, yet with congruent values with the state of Vermont. Very comfortable in this tranquil and uncomplicated and nature abundant setting. Healthy food and lifestyle. Good values based on plain common sense and decency. Coming home to where it all began; lakes, mountains, streams, winding country roads, foliage, rainy and snowy days. Our ancestors all came from this heritage, in England and Scotland (Germany too).

This is our natural circadian rhythm. I feel so at home here. I feel peace. It is correct for me. I am provided precious solitude and alone time when I desire and need it. My wife has friends and family so she feels connected and safe. Her family are seventh generation Vermonters. She is truly home! We each can have our own time, together and apart. This is healthy and necessary for growth. As I age, I desire more time to think, remember, process, and reflect. To loosely make plans too, when needed. I am feeling comfortable, satisfied, and content where I find myself now. Serenity lives here for me.

Challenges are different now in some ways, but I find little stress because I have been there so many times before in my life. This is familiar territory for me and I feel confident I can transform any future "bumps" into another positive growth opportunity and learning experience. The challenges in life and our responses to them are so affirming to the state of being truly alive! Be an active participant in your own life! How blessed are we who live truly alive really are! It is up to each of us to be fully engaged in this wondrous gift from God. Thank you God! Amen.

ESSAY 11:
The Need for Connections, from mortal to eternal

What are connections and why are they essential in human existence? When we are born, we need to be connected to our mothers. They provide safety, nourishment, security, and comfort. This need is primal. We are totally dependent on that connection for our very survival. So it is throughout the entire animal kingdom. The connection soon extends to our fathers, then our siblings, our family, our relatives. Soon enough we seek connections with our friends and schoolmates. Then in our communities and at work.

The point is, we want and need to belong to something bigger than ourselves. It validates us. Human beings are social animals. We want to be part of the larger group. We want to be included, not excluded. As we progress through life, family relationships can change. We may go in different directions, develop different interests, live different lives and may have different values. We can drift apart, thus the connection is weakened or even severed. The same is true with friends and in the workplace. Being social, we seek different connections along our pathways of life. But it seems we never want to be without some connection to someone or someplace or some other thing that has been significant in our life. These connections are essential to who we are.

And some may reach the point where they dare ask themselves, who am I? What and who am I connected to that has been with me my entire life? Who will be with me to my final days and beyond? Who have I always had a connection to, since my first breath? I did not know it then, but I have lived long enough to come to the realization that the only connection that lasts forever is the connection to my Maker, God! He is the only connector that really matters. Others come and go in our lifetimes. He was with us before our birth and will remain connected to us through all eternity.

So it seems to me that to come to recognize and embrace this concept of true connection is to understand the Oneness of all that is. We are all connected, to Him and to everything that exists in all the universes and all thru eternity. We are connected to before and after this present incarnation. When a person can really grasp this concept, he can see and know that he will always have a connection to something much larger than himself. He will always belong. Thus, he will always be safe, nourished, secure and comforted, forever. He is never alone, nor has he ever been.

ESSAY 12:
Troubles

What are "troubles"? Life is full of varying degrees of troubles. We all have them. They can be minor. They can be major. How do we best deal with them? How we perceive them can influence how we choose to confront them. Do we ignore them and look the other way, hope and pray they just disappear? Do we put off handling them? Do we fear them? Do we deny their existence as long as possible? Do we run from them, try to escape via drugs and alcohol and other means of avoidance?

I would dare suggest a novel way to deal with life's troubles. If one can reach a certain point of spiritual awareness and development, it can be possible to grow beyond your troubles. You can do this by separating yourself from the troubles before you. By accepting the fact that troubles do exist and looking at them from a detached point of view, you can lessen the burden upon yourself. Yes, these do exist but they are not MY troubles. per se. These are troubles that must be dealt with but by detaching from them on a spiritual level, you can remove your direct involvement in them. By that, I mean that distancing yourself frees you to be less emotionally involved and attached to a particular outcome.

By distancing yourself and looking at the situation from way above, you gain perspective. You can remove your emotions, your fears, your uncertainty and doubts. You can take some time and carefully dissect and analyze what is at hand. By becoming more calm and less attached, you can see much more clearly. A course of action will reveal itself soon enough and by being willing to flow with your messages, you will eventually choose the correct path for you. The correct path may not appear so initially but all will be resolved as it is meant to be.

In learning to look at adverse events in life from a distance, the action required will reveal itself more clearly to you and you will become much more confident in your responses. You will become stronger and more trusting in yourself. You will learn to be more patient and observant and become much better equipped to handle all the trials living a life successfully requires. You are truly growing yourself from each test you successfully navigate through. You are becoming the forever student as you learn to accept and be mentored by the forever teacher, your Divine God. And all is well, always.

ESSAY 13:
Alignment

When one goes deep within and truly connects with one's inner truth, he is aligning with the creative energy process that God makes available to all via that individual's specific efforts to seek out, identify, and embrace and trust this energy. You are actually aligning with yourself through Him. You become stronger, more serene, and centered as this alignment increases. The energy potentiates and you become more comfortable with an increasing peace of mind. You become more in tune with the Divine order where uncertainty and fear cease to exist. Chaos disappears and you grow to marvel, appreciate, trust, accept, grow and evolve. And it, of necessity, comes from the inside, where your own Divinity, by design, resides all along.

It is perpetual and you are merely tapping into it on this brief Earthly visit. It is, has been, and always will be ongoing- eternal. It is like a butterfly who finally learns to trust the wind and just taps into that energy and travels to where the wind takes him. That insect quits fighting it and just relaxes and enjoys the ride and the place it lands is where the butterfly is supposed to be. Very wise and so natural.

It all works. Mortal humans are always seeking something and fighting against everything to get what they "want". Not what they need for most everyone has what they need. All we should strive to be doing is to tap into that Devine inner energy life force and accept and enjoy the brief journey. Peace of mind is a choice, it is priceless and it is there all along- for free!

THE POINT OF LIFE.....is to align your inner soul energy frequency to God's frequency and therefore, Thus, I am...ONE! To come to Oneself and align! This may only be accomplished by honoring your own God-given truth. With such an inner connection, the actions of others do not really matter. World events do not shake you. You become more disengaged from externals and more in tune with your internals. They nourish you and you will come to discover strong connections with other persons of personal integrity and similar values. These persons will be attracted to you and you to them via being on the same vibrational energy frequency. Their vibrations will resonate with yours and life becomes more meaningful and joyous. Your and their energies will potentiate each other.

Just like spontaneous combustion, when a stack of old oily rags generates enough heat to initiate a smoldering tiny flame, that flame erupts into a large fire. This could be the eruption from the spark that is growing within you as you start to recognize that energy within and you connect with other like individuals. The energy grows stronger and becomes a force that you embrace and grow and nurture for the rest of your life. I must again emphasize that the spark HAS to arise WITHIN YOU before you can be aware of it in others.

Again, this is an INDIVIDUAL process, unique to each person who discovers this process. It is unique to each person for each person is on his own spiritual journey to live his own truth. It has to be an internal process and it is thus impossible to receive your answers externally from other persons. It is, of necessity, a solitary journey to go within for your connection and answers, but one is not alone. You feel God's guidance as the connection strengthens. But, one will come to recognize and be attracted to others on a similar journey of personal enlightenment. You will find yourself disengaging from negative people, events and thoughts. You will seek out the good and the beauty will draw you in, naturally and effortlessly. Life will become a joyous experience filled with wonderment, appreciation and so much learning, despite all the obstacles confronted along the way. Life is truly good.

ESSAY 14:
Aaron Rogers and Awareness...Metaphor for Life

Watching Aaron Rogers play football is such a treat! He looks at the existing situation as the defense presents it to him. He then figures out how to counter this alignment and makes the proper adjustments and takes action to make the most of what is there. He just KNOWS he will figure it out. He will do it, whatever is needed. Concerned, perhaps at times, but never panic. He is prepared. When one is prepared, you may feel pressure, but you do not experience stress. Stress occurs when one is not prepared. Aaron just has this awareness! Observing his confidence is an excellent metaphor for life!

We are all at our own levels. They are all different and unique to each of us. You and I are on different awareness levels. Period. This is a non-judgmental statement of fact. I respect that and accept that and understand that. One does not judge. It does not mean they are less than we are. It does mean they are at a different place than we are.

Always keeping this thought in mind, there is never a cause or need to ever pass judgement on another. "Hey, he is where he is. I respect that. "Recognizing and acknowledging this defuses any feelings of anger, sadness, or frustration. It is simply "what it is". Live and let live.

Be responsible for your own circumstance and growth and detach from the path of others.

This is where they are, accept it. Their journey. This is not a contest with others. Perhaps with oneself, however. Not a competition. This is a quest, an individual one, by definition and of necessity.

Thus, I am calm. I feel very centered, very connected...with ONE.

ESSAY 15:
The Hereafter...An Analogy

Imagine if you were born and grew up never being able to taste, smell, hear, feel, speak or see. Really think about and absorb this concept in its totality. You have never, ever experienced any of these sensations. Then, as a young adult, you woke up one morning and suddenly, you could experience all these for the first time in your life!!! Could you ever find adequate words to describe the overwhelming pure joy and wonderment of being exposed to the full world of using these sensations and know you would be able to enjoy these senses for the rest of your life!? You would be in pure bliss!! Utopia!! Everything is now possible you would believe. You truly are experiencing heaven on Earth!

I am of the opinion this is exactly what one would experience when one crosses over into the highest realm of total ONE, except it would be one trillion plus times more profound! It would be infinitely more encompassing in all possible ways! Life on this planet we live on could be compared in very primitive simplicity to a single grain of sand vs. the complexity of a human brain operating on all cylinders, or a planet full of computers all operating at the same time in their calculations. Not even close. Dimensions so very, very far beyond our simple and very basic, five senses.

What could there possibly be to fear? Rather, this is to be viewed as a humongous graduation event! Job well done! ...ONWARD!!! ...

ESSAY 16:
Expectations

I have no expectations of anybody, except those I have for myself. It is not fair to expect anybody to do what you think they "should" do. They will do what they want or feel they need to do, for them, period. For me, when people do not meet what I have expected of them, it is a opportunity for me to learn who and what they really are. Who am I to judge them? They are on their journey and I am on mine. I will say that I observe and take note of what their actions are. These actions speak volumes to me about where they are in this life. Who are they, really? Then I know, for I observe, study, deduce and discover. This empowers me and informs me and grows me.

This feeling of "knowing" empowers me to do what I need to do in handling these types of people. I can release them as not players on the same field I am presently on. Also, I can recognize true spiritual beings and learn from them. Again, what fascinating lessons are to be learned in living a challenging and stimulating life! Who would want to spend years in dormant situations simply waiting to die?

Personally, I have observed that the lazy ones, the "safe" ones, the underachievers, the establishment ones who played the game and got their final "reward" of financial security by playing along to get along are the real losers in this life. Why, you may ask? Because they never took the risk of entering the arena of life where you alone were totally responsible for your very own survival. You lacked the character to trust and allow yourself to be tested because it was "safer" to avoid the test altogether.

For me personally, I would much rather be in the company of those who took risks, even if not successful, than those who lived the safe life. The dreamers who dare risk all for those dreams are my true heroes, not those who play it safe and "win". Win what? At what cost? How does a risk-free life grow you spiritually? With no personal hardships or suffering, how does one learn compassion for others? What was the point?

ESSAY 17:
The Sun, and It's Lessons

Today, I was able to sit in the sun at 4 pm. I was very tired after working all day on things at my new dental office. I sat in the recliner lounge chair and tipped back. I was facing the sun and I closed my eyes. I took a deep release sigh and exhaled. I felt the sun in my eyes with them being closed. What was I feeling at that very moment? I instantly felt at total and absolute peace. It was such a deep and resolute sense of release. A surrender. A connection. I was One with the sun. One must pay attention and I always try to do just that. At this moment, I was totally present.

I was starving for the sun. When I allowed myself to be totally in that moment, I knew. It was so awesome. I have always known that when our time on Earth is done, we are drawn to the light. In the light, all our troubles and concerns just cease to be in our awareness. They do not matter. God speaks to us all, in so many ways. I always listen. He is telling us that all is OK. He has our back.

The light of Heaven, which I previewed today, will be to the Nth degree so much more than the sun I experienced today! It is just so affirming in all manner possible. It is quantum beyond human comprehension. What a spectacular future that awaits us all! I just feel so blessed that I had this brief preview today. And I could see the gift. Like the sun, the Light will draw you in and you will feel safe and you will want more. It is all just so right!

ESSAY 18:
Life Throughout All The Universe

When one looks at the literal billions and billions of types and forms and variety of life just on this single planet, how can one not even imagine that the same thing also exists throughout all the planets that support some form of life in all the universe? It is just so evident to me that the designs that produce all this infinite variety have to be Divine! I am absolutely convinced of this, beyond all doubt. It is as obvious as the presence of the sun is obvious.

I find such absolute comfort in the belief and conviction of this. It just makes perfect sense. There is absolutely zero chance that such an organized and perfect system could all just be happenstance! Just look all around you and see all the variety before your very eyes! And it is all by design, not by accident at all. The more one studies and observes all these phenomena around us, the more convinced any thinking person must become. We are so puny, so tiny, so minor, so not significant, even for those who truly can see and believe the divinity of all things.

For the life forms that can see and believe, there is more ahead for them. For they appreciate what they know and feel and believe and for them comes acceptance, trust, and peace of mind, in this lifetime and beyond. Such surrender brings so many rewards and clarifies and enhances one's experiences here on Earth and for what may come next. How can one fear what is "next" when you have total trust and belief in the order and perfection of what is? Perfection does exist and it is all around you. The system is flawless and it fills me with wonder and curiosity and excitement even, as I can only imagine what splendor awaits all of those who truly can see.

Such statements are not at all originating from arrogance. I am smart enough to know that what I do know is nothing! We all know nothing! I also believe that few people think as I do. They find my comments and thoughts leave them rather speechless. They just have nothing much to say. I conclude that they have a different awareness than I. Not less, not more, just different.

That is OK because I can only identify with how I believe. It is my total independent, solitary, and unique life and I choose to examine this miracle in my own way. It seems to me that not many people really go very deep with this. I cannot help myself, for I am wired this way. I just need to try to figure things out. And I make my attempts knowing that many things cannot be figured out. They just are. I can live with that. But I try as best I am capable of.

I find that as I continue to examine, observe, and reach my conclusions, I achieve a great sense of connection. It is so gratifying and validating to my being, that I am a part of something so magnificent in the whole. I find myself just marveling at the miracle of all this life in all its forms, all around me. I do not understand how people cannot address these questions. Maybe most do but I have serious doubts about this. I have not found anyone who even tries to go as deep on this as I do. I know some do, but I know of none personally. Again, we are all on our own separate paths in life. We view things so differently.

I feel that people who do not make these connections are depriving themselves of great opportunities for growth. They fail to see all the evidence, sense the connections, and thus live with no core bedrock beliefs or real faith, no lasting peace of mind and the calm that comes from this. They tend to needlessly or continually worry, rather than just be a bit concerned from time to time. They fail to comprehend that everything is temporary. They tend to get all upset and caught up in the routines and events of living and fail to take the time to really see all that can be seen, if they really look.

There is a calmness that can be achieved under most any circumstance when a person can detach and look down upon it from a great distance, be it time or space. Then the circumstance may be reframed and more properly and easily dealt with. Nobody gives a damn now and in 50 years, they most certainly will not give a damn either. Only you can give a damn and make the effort to achieve this serenity, for you, in your lifetime. It is your work and it only matters to you and it should matter to you. Thus, it is actually all about you, in this sense.

ESSAY 19:

Peachland Beach, BC... Awareness, in the Moment

I am sitting here in the grass, enjoying the afternoon shade of a cottonwood tree on a sunny summer day feeling a cool breeze off a gorgeous and tranquil Lake Okanagan. I am viewing the mountains across the lake and the blue sky and soft gentle cumulus clouds above. My spirit is alive and well. Cyclically, when I am not "doing" but rather "being", I am feeling centered and peaceful and so totally at ease. I am in a serene place, spiritually and physically. I am acutely aware that I am "of the world" and not so much "in the world".

I am detached from the madness and frenzy and go within to that God-like spiritual and peaceful place that radiates from inside out. I do not need or seek the "external" for I have abundance from the "internal." I have no more external wants for I am full enough from within. I have most all my answers for me and external questions are of no concern to me. I drop out by going within.

From within, I find all my answers. I do not seek or need to look externally for my answers. My truth resides within me. No one can presume to tell me my truths. My gift is to go deeper within myself. The challenge, and it has been an easy one, is to be able to ID the places and circumstances by which I supply the environment to better do this. That is why one has to create safe and simple sanctuaries. Close to nature, free of "clutter". Sane places to fill my spirit and feed my soul.

For me, some of those places have been the lake cabin, RC home on Rapid Creek, Mendocino, Peachland, BC, Windsor homestead on the Conn. R., Sedona, Palm Springs, Lucerne Switzerland, Key Largo, Anna Maria Island, Fl. Mountains, water, clear skies and nights, nature, animals, fireplace, solitude and quiet. Also, I have discovered, now easily for me, that all I really need is to go deep within my own mind. I fill myself from within first, thus I always have a safe place of peace and order and sense of things. I can direct and control everything there. Eventually, I can access precise clarity of thought, direction and action, when needed. I need only to reside there from time to time to keep my sanity and creative juices flowing.

I have discovered that the spirit of God leads me to light. Thus, I may become enlightened by that "Aha" moment, that sudden clarity that bursts forth with a new idea and inspiration. Also, I always strive to live in His light by living by His rules rather than by man's rules. I aspire to this.

Nihilism.......I can find myself becoming bored and empty if I am not being creative and taking some action on a regular enough basis. I need to be doing something "productive" from time to time. How much sitting, reading and playing can I do before I begin losing my edge and begin sinking in mind and spirit? I need to have meaning in my life. Thus, I must seek BALANCE between being inside for meditation and clarity and venturing outside for action. This works for me. The challenge becomes, what works for you? Discover this for yourself and you shall be forever free. Truly living a liberated life!

ESSAY 20:
Genesis of Life on Earth

I believe that our answers are all around us. A fact is that a mighty oak tree can arise from a single tiny seed. All the "codes and directions" for that oak tree to develop and flourish are there waiting to be unleashed. So too with all life forms, humans included. One single celled sperm fertilizes one single cell egg. Out of that "simple" fusion the codes are set in motion. Every single function is set in motion to differentiate into specific cells that all have their "assignments". Thus, a heart, a finger, a toenail, a liver, a brain, etc. etc. Everything just develops according to plan.

Thus it is with the genesis of initial life on earth, in my opinion, i.e. the big picture of all these billions of life forms on planet earth. It began with the "seeding" of this round spinning sphere that was just the correct distance from this sun to support these forms of life. With an endless and forever expanding universe, of course there is life teeming everywhere.

What is so difficult to believe about the likelihood of a meteor from a distant galaxy containing the seeds necessary to initiate life in all its forms on this planet we now occupy? It is the same methodology from which all life is initiated. Sperm and egg. The meteor was the sperm that fertilized the egg named Earth. Then differentiation began that evolved into all the forms of life we now have. Just as the oak tree differentiates and human tissues are created and form all the complex functions and structures that make us human. It is all coded from that initial union.

So, life on earth is no accident, not even close! However, such events most likely have happened on many other planets but the "impregnating" did not work because the conditions were not conducive to supporting life as we know it. However, I am 100% certain that multitudes of "earths" exist throughout the vast galaxies. I do not believe life simply arose from nothing. The supposition that evolution is just pure happenstance left solely to chance is not viable to my way of thinking. Everything is just too perfect. Evolution does exist but it has guidance. Why have so much variety in everything and it is all so precise and exact? God makes everything so obvious and it is right in front of us. HE leaves clues to those who are curious or seeking, everywhere!

Take fractals. The presence of these geometric patterns in all forms of life and nature just reinforces the divine and orderly laws of nature. These designs cannot just be an accident. They exist in all the photos of the universe, in snowflakes, in tree branches, leaves, sand dunes, shorelines, ocean waves, size and arrangement of teeth, radio frequencies, etc, etc. Everywhere!!

Thus, nothing is happenstance! Everything is by design. Life on earth and throughout the cosmos in all its forms is by design. And it's beginnings are by design, for as I have stated, everything is in the codes that dictate the totality of all existence. In a similar manner, I do not believe that a "Big Bang" initiated the universe. We humans always believe that everything must have a "beginning". But to have a beginning is to accept that the universe would also have an ending. The universe is expanding!

To have a start and a finish is to believe that the concept of time really exists. But we know we can view events in the universe in our earthly present moment that happened in the far distant past. Yet, we can see them in our present "time." So what is time, really? In the universe there is no such thing as time. That is a necessary concept that humans invented so they could reference things. The universe is timeless for it has no beginning and has no end, so time as a concept, is not valid to me, in the grand scheme of things.

When we pass on from our brief lives on earth, we will be ONE with all "before" us and all "after" us, for everything remains ONE. As stated in previous essays, every form and entity and creature are all just energy, which cannot be created or destroyed, it only changes in form. The oneness of all the energy from everything in the universe is a constant. So the concept of time is just that - a concept. That does not address the concept of a soul. That is a separate topic. That is all about consciousness and that has been discussed in other essays.

ESSAY 21:
Infinity, and Beyond

Yes, I am currently named Jack Howard Weaver. What does that mean, really?? I am who? I am a male. I am beyond being a male. I am beyond female. I am beyond human. I am actually an equal to all forms that exist, for I am but a tiny portion of the TOTAL with no real definition or identity in language terms. Identity is just a name we humans give everything so we can label it and thus conceive of it. I am ALL and I am ONE, with all energy in all the universes for all infinity.

Thus, I do not actually exist as Jack Weaver, per se. I am so way beyond being that entity. For I, like everything that has form or does not have form, exist as energy, pure and simple. As energy, my physical form may be "destroyed", but it is simply altered into some other frequency or part of the infinite energy field. I am the same as a grain of sand, or as a drop of water. No difference at all when you break it all down to beyond the smallest unit of energy. Way smaller than subatomic. Smaller than neutrinos. Smaller than quarks.

ANALOGY...The ocean as the universe. The ocean is referred to as "endless". It exists forever all over our planet. The ocean exists as water. The water nourishes all life in the ocean and on all lands. Water evaporates, ie. it changes form, from a liquid to a gas. The vapor goes into the atmosphere as a gas, it cools, it coalesces into a droplet and falls again to the earth as rain. It may fall into the ocean again. It may fall into a stream and be taken far from whence it came to earth this time. It may fall to the ground. No matter where it falls, it is in a different place from whence it was the last time it fell to earth. It may nourish a plant, which is eaten by an animal, which is eaten by a human, who eliminates waste from that food which was processed in that body. That waste will nourish the land and that land will produce nutrients that will give off gases and byproducts. This, in turn, will affect other systems of life.

So, the point is, that simple drop of water will have changed form and supported all forms of life forever. It will never cease to exist, at least the atoms that comprise the gases that make it up will not ever cease to exist. Thus it is with "Jack Weaver " or whomever or whatever label we are assigned or borrow in this endless continuum throughout all eternity.

ESSAY 22:

The Narrative and the Scam... The Way America Works and the Sales Pitch for Creating and Selling Perpetual Wars...Part One

The special interests of American capitalists identify what they want. They do not care one damn about the country they reside in. They care only about making as much money and acquiring and exerting as much power as that money can buy in perpetuating their self-serving agenda. Using oil as an example. They "negotiate" with any country they suspect has something that will make them a lot of money. They "cut a deal" with the "rulers" of that country. If it is a dictator, so much the better. If not, they can arrange that the representative government be overthrown so they can install their chosen ruler. Think the Shaw of Iran when oil was the focus there in the 50's. The established government of Iran was overthrown and a US. Govt. (owned by special interests) chosen "ruler" (US puppet dictator) was installed with America's ie, special interests blessings. The US declares this person an important ally and "friend" of the USA and thus justifies sending US arms and money to "support" our new USA ally. This person will protect us against our "enemies" in the region.

This puppet dictator uses our tax money sent to him to purchase our weapons to use against his "enemies" ie, his own people, who now become enemies of the USA, because their actions are not in the true interests of the US. That is, not in the interests of our special interests who really control our government. So the commonality here is that money and power rule in every single country in existence. The powerful rule and dominate the weak in every country where money is to be made and people are to be exploited and marginalized to meet this end.

This applies everywhere USA capitalism can reach. Actually, it is happening all over the world. Major capitalist interests are now so powerful that they exist far beyond governments. They have more influence and more power than any government has at the present time. I choose to focus on the USA but it happens everywhere, because people are people. So, here is the BS narrative. We need to sell the American people that we have enemies out there. There always must be an enemy. Of course, we have created these enemies by supporting and sponsoring oppression of the true wishes of these people who are now ruled by dictators we have installed to suppress them for our gain rather than theirs.

So we have this concept of foreign aid. It is packaged as helping the less fortunate of other countries. Thus, the good empathic US citizens would support such a noble purpose. They buy it. However, it is so much more. It is purchasing loyalty and support from other countries who need this US tax money to keep all their pockets lined. The hell with the people! It buys silence. It buys UN votes. It buys good PR. It lines lots of pockets and rewards dictators and tyrants for keeping their people in line so they do not rebel against their oppressive governments so far removed from what their people want and need. The US owns these leaders and their citizens know it!

So voila! Perfect set-up for selling the entire war agenda! These people who live in foreign countries and are ruled by proxy via US sponsored "governments" become angry and eventually desperate. Think Palestine and US sponsored Israel. Or Saudi Arabia and the entire Middle East. These people hate the US because we sponsor and support their oppressors and rape their country and it's natural resources. We introduce our values and beliefs into their culture. We become disruptive to their customs and way of life. We become a threat to everything they stand for. Why would they not hate us? We exploit everything about them!

So what do people with no hope do? What do people who are miserable with zero control in their lives do? Are they not ripe for exploitation by sinister forces who have a totally different overall agenda? These forces can recruit easily because they can offer an honorable way out. They can promise an escape via martyrdom and celestial virgins and rewards beyond all belief! What young and impressionable and devout person would not jump at this glorious opportunity to serve his master? And to take as many non-believers with him as possible? It is a very quick and simple solution to an impossible situation.

So there you have it. The SI (special interests) now have complete control....... Part Two to Follow.

ESSAY 23:
Special Interests and War... Part Two

OK, we now have enemies with a name. You have to have an enemy with a name so you can effectively create fear. Fear sells. And who will protect you from this new threat? Why, your protector, your government of course! But there must be sacrifices by the people. More on that later. It changes from decade to decade but we must name these enemies before we can sell the need to destroy them. Today, it is the War on Terror". Who are these terrorists?

These are presented as enemies of the US who want to take away our freedoms and destroy our way of life. So not true! These are simply people who want us to get out of their lives and their countries and leave them alone. They hate us because of the misery our actions have brought upon them. Of course, many want to get even. They want to hurt us like we have hurt them. And they could care less about dying in the fight. After all, have not we or our sponsored activities killed many of their innocent loved ones? Why not join them in death and take as many perpetrators with you as possible?

Of course, we have been responsible for so many innocent deaths. Why would not a surviving victim also desire to kill innocent people of all the countries who sponsor these activities against them? Makes perfect sense for a desperate suffering victim our actions have created. So, our Corporate owned government needs to create a reason to "protect our people and way of life." Naturally, our corporations who benefit directly from all these shenanigans have no intention of paying one single dime for reaping all these profits they gain from their exploitation of others. They pay no taxes, they hide their money and they always want more.

Not to worry. Their purchased politicians protect them. And these politicians are in turn rewarded by funding from these same entities whom they support monetarily to keep them in office. Thus, our leaders tell us of this grave threat out there. Of course, we created this very threat. So, we demand more money in our defense budget. We need bombers, fighter jets, aircraft carriers, tanks, helicopters, drones, ground troops, submarines, etc, etc, to fight enemies with turbans and sandals in a giant sand box.

No matter that massive and obscene amount of money could rebuild every highway, school, bridge, and hospital in the entire country. But how could corporate America profit? Look at the loss of profit from arms sales, defense contractors, military bases, etc. We need to spend that money on defense rather than our own infrastructure for how else can we continue to exploit these other countries unless we spend the necessary funds to continue to do so? Priorities are very important and our national "defense "must always be priority number one!

OK. To protect our country and it's "interests", we need soldiers. With no draft how do we attract these people? So many ways. You create a system that eliminates opportunity for adequate education and job training. You outsource jobs to other countries who pay less. With no costly and burdensome regulations to deal with in other countries, corporate America saves billions. So what that we ship jobs overseas, it helps our bottom line. To hell with what is good for our country and society, greed rules over all else.

Our politicians also enable a huge drug crisis to sweep the nation. This further erodes our social fabric. We encourage video games sales that promote war and violence in the minds of our youth. We encourage Hollywood and TV to make and promote war movies. We advertise the attractive "team player" concept to make it sound very appealing to join the military team and defend your country. We actively recruit in high schools, depressed neighborhoods, and other environments that we have created a need to escape from. Thus, we manufacture the very situations that deny opportunities to our young people and then offer them a way out to further our national (corporate) interests that created the situation in the first place! How ironic and convenient is that?!

So, these young people join the military in order to improve their lives by escaping all the circumstances of their current situations. They are then brainwashed further by the military system and made pawns by our leaders. They are being used and becoming trained killers courtesy of the peace loving USA. These new soldiers have good intentions. They take the bait of defending their country. They are true patriots. They make America and their families proud. Some even die for their country and are celebrated as hero's. And they are heroes. Their sacrifices are real. But the reasons they are trained and forced to fight are all bogus!

Some soldiers figure it out. In my opinion, Exhibit A is Pat Tillman. He joined the military for all the right reasons, in his mind. When he started to write home with his observations of being duped and now figuring the entire game out, he was "killed in combat." Of course, the circumstances of his death were falsified and he was portrayed as a hero who died a glorious death on the battlefield saving his fellow soldiers. He was being used yet again by the powers that be. I believe the truth is he was fracked by his own men. He was a potential threat to the national narrative. His death was a set-up, even if the killing soldier was not aware of it. The circumstance of his death was created by his commanding officers even if they did not pull the trigger. And the beat goes on, and on, and on. Creating carnage and misery all over the world.

ESSAY 24:

The psychology of the military and government... Part Three..FINIS!!

The systems in place and the powers that be are very clever. Government policies of destroying social fabric, promoting violence, eliminating educational opportunities, sowing distrust, divisiveness, increasing joblessness, etc, etc are all directed to weaken our society and serve the special interests rather than our own people. We sell to these trapped young people the "opportunities" the military can offer. A huge thing the military does is that it promotes the teamwork concept because it knows the value of this.

The soldier fights more for his comrades in arms than for the policies of its government at that particular time. Wounded soldiers want to return to battle because his buddies need him. Do not let your buddy down is a powerful draw. It sucks you right back in. Survivors carry that guilt for their entire lifetimes. Too many choose death by suicide to escape the pain. Those who die for the cause are told "thank you" from a grateful nation. You have made the ultimate sacrifice for your appreciative nation. And families need to hear this and believe that their country honors their sacrifice and their death means something bigger than them.

The sad fact is that their death or sacrifice was indeed necessary to serve the "bigger good." It was a supreme price to pay and it needs to be honored for these pour souls who have suffered with honor. It cannot mean nothing. Tragically, what it means is that your loved one was used and you have been used by your government. And your government is bought and paid for by the special interests of this country. And your good old government who sucked you into this entire mess will discard you like an old pair of shoes when you are no longer useful to them. Veterans' needs are sorely neglected. Almost no opportunities exist for them after their service, same as before it.

These sinister forces have become a malignancy that has spread worldwide. Citizens have less and less control and special interests have most all control now. The government creates the problem, it sells it to the populace, it dictates the solution and forces that upon a reluctant nation. Actually, enough people believe the story that little prevents it from being the official version of truth. Dissenters are marginalized and discredited. They are traitors who do not go along to get along. They are not true patriots.

War will always exist in America. We will continue our ways until we have destroyed our planet. It is as it always has been. Man does not change. We want something someone else has. We are more powerful than they are. As our former VP Dick Chaney once stated, "What good is power if you don't use it?" Well, we use it. We take what we want from whomever and they fight us back. The saga is accelerating on all fronts. Critical mass is now. Never ending until the end! America is greater than ever! We won!??

ESSAY 25:
Life Flow, till the end

I believe we are evaluated (don't like word judged) by how well we meet and handle the struggles that we face and endure during our lifetime. Some people are just pitted against horrific circumstances from birth. Some people have defective DNA that predisposes them to extreme medical conditions. These can lead to a shortened life span, one with daily pain and daunting challenges. If we fight as hard as we can in life with these conditions and we eventually become just completely depleted in body and mind, we eventually succumb and pass on.

I believe God rewards us for fighting the good battle to the end. He will liberate us and we are finally free of all pain and suffering. We are now perfect and our previous life is but a distant blink. Like a snake shedding his skin, it is discarded and totally forgotten about. Who among us thinks one second about discarding cut hair or fingernails? We move on without a thought.

We are on a continuum and all of us are exposed, challenged, and stimulated in different ways. Ultimately, we all end up as ONE, and the process continues forever. No beginning and no end thru eternity. Personally, I am very comfortable with that, totally. It is all so perfect. Now when innocent children or anybody is taken through zero causes of their own, I believe God readily accepts them and they live forever with no Earthly concerns. They may come back or they may transcend to another place where life is more loving and fair. I do feel they are very well taken care of.

I do believe that just being given life and being born is a supreme gift from God and there are no guarantees. Things will and do happen. When the innocent die, I feel this is a supreme test for those who loved them. Do they trust in God and surrender to the result without anger and hate and loss of faith? Do they turn against God, rather than love Him more, knowing their loved one is in His loving hands forever? Do they thank God for being graced with this precious loved one in their life for as long as they were? For most everyone, this is a most severe test of all tests.

Again, I must state that man causes this misery on Earth, not God. God deals with the aftermath. I do also believe God sometimes intervenes and brings justice in a person's lifetime. He may also save someone from peril whom He feels has more work to do. The point is, nobody knows for certain. But, there are signs all around us if we take the time to look. God's work and His perfect design is everywhere. It really is a magnificently designed system that is continually self-correcting to maintain the balance. Man will try his utmost to destroy it but if/when he does, God will restore the balance again. Probably take thousands of years, but the plan will be as it is supposed to be. It always is and accepting this fact totally, brings me great peace.

ESSAY 26:
Energy, Internal and Eternal

All in the universe is energy. Everything in this and on this Earth and everywhere in the universe is energy at the smallest neutrino level with space existing between each particle. And energy cannot be created or destroyed, it can only change in form. Thus, the first rule of thermodynamics and it is irrefutable, just like gravity is a fact of the universe. Period! There is a frequency for everything and a special wavelength that is of the "ONE", the human-God connection. T

To me, the task and goal of life is to tune into that energy that is of the "ONE". A mortal human discovers and lives his life on an energy continuum and part of that specific energy flow of I am... ONE. One and the same, for zero separation exists. The task of living as a mortal, on that same energy level, is to become aware of that and live on this earth in human form on that same frequency as.. I am... ONE.

Be aware of it, identify it, become conscious of it, feel it, cultivate it, and celebrate it! That is the true mission and purpose of this life on Earth. Thus, one lives in heaven (energy wise) while on earth. Discover and feel the true vibration of the heavenly life in your mortal form and you are evolving and becoming...ONE, while on earth. Nothing else matters when this state is achieved. Peace and serenity and connectedness emanate from your soul while in an earthly form.

It is ONE'S life, not your own. Release, trust, surrender, discover, marvel, celebrate, enjoy and accept the ultimate truth and plan of what is. It has absolutely zero to do with you in the human form. It is all the same universal energy, vibrating at different frequencies. Like a radio station, TV, cell phone, etc. When tuned in properly, specific things happen. You are always being spoken to, IF you are truly listening!

ESSAY 27:
Skeeters and Skimmers

Skeeters are the name that was used, in my youth, to describe surface insects that darted in zig-zags across the surface of pond water. They existed only on the surface. They were in the sun and rain and wind only on the surface. They were totally unaware of all the events that existed below the surface they spent their brief lives upon.

So too, is it with the vast majority of human beings. They live entirely on the surface of everything. They do not know or care about what happens at the deeper levels. Everything that seems important and relevant to them exists only within their narrow world upon the surface. They spend their entire lives there, unconsciously, for all sorts of reasons. They examine little, question little, are conscious of little. They are born, live on the surface, pass on to oblivion for all they know.

In my observations, even many intelligent persons are not motivated or conscious enough to even attempt to truly examine below this surface. They may be considered "smart", yet they are ignorant of what really matters. The awareness is just not there. I truly believe that I am aware. At least I make the attempt. I am a keen observer, an examiner, ask the questions and I seek my answers, from within. Thus, for me, I am beyond many others, yet this is in no way a competition, for me. Nor do I view myself as "superior" in any way. Just different, on my own path. This is a personal and individual quest I have been on my entire life.

So, many people just do not comprehend where my thinking and beliefs come from. They are so not aware that they could never possibly grasp what I am all about. They may have fame, wealth, or power, but, as I see it, they still do get the true picture. Their reality is entirely superficial. Thus, "whom" they are means nothing to me–zero, zilch, natta. They do not count. To me, it is they who do not "get it", not me. I find peace of mind and strong conviction that my perceptions make sense to me. That is all that really matters in my world, beneath the surface, where true growth, development, and life and "death" are defined at the soul level.

ESSAY 28:
Kathy Ireland "observation"

A former supermodel, now a successful entrepreneur, she states "When I was young, I had this shy, quiet shell. As I grew older, I learned to get over this protective shield in able to accomplish what I wanted from life." (JW, from here, adds his twist to the gist of her message). We must never be ruled by fear. We must dare, take risks, reach out and make the required effort. Do not permit comfort or convenience to short circuit us. Do not take the safer, more secure, or easier way, if it means you will be predisposed to fall short. Be careful, for it is insidious. Unfortunately for most, it becomes their way of life.

You must force yourself, often many times, to venture out of your comfort zone. With each test of this, you will gain much in strength and confidence. These attributes, in turn, drive you forward with determination and a reinforced sense of purpose. Opportunities will reveal themselves to you. Embrace them, seize them! Figure out what you want and make it happen. Always dream fearlessly! In seeking out new opportunities, ask questions. When someone says No, the question is Why? When someone says Yes, the question is ``How?"

I have added some of my views into her narrative but I do agree with her 100%! That is why she continues to be successful in her life. I greatly respect people such as her!

ESSAY 29:
Proclivities

Most people have no plan and just bounce around throughout life. They do not think, they react, a big difference. They respond to stimuli like a simple brainless organism, like a basic worm or caterpillar that recoils when touched. People encounter obstacles and rather than meet the challenge, they seek the easy way, the most comfortable way to avoid making the effort. They concede, they compromise, they settle.

Some will do this until they recognize the price, but most do not even examine this. What is the price? The cost is you surrender your power. You back down from the Divine challenge that we all should, but very few, even recognize. The challenge is to dare try to achieve all the God given potentials we are all born with. We are born and then our tests begin.

Proclivities are tendencies to behave in certain ways in direct response to certain situations, circumstances, or stimuli. SIDE NOTE... A person in their ego will refer to an accomplishment of another, as "my son, my husband, my dear friend, whatever" did so and so. Thus, it becomes a focus upon them for they are trying too hard to get reflected glory from the other person via directing their accomplishments through a connection to them! Now it is about them! Very selfish, self-directed and sad. It shows a deep insecurity and need for recognition. And perhaps even a deep need for love and acceptance.

ESSAY 30:
The Soul Of Man, Part One of Two

Love is what it is all about. Love of God, love of self, love of others, love of animals, love of life. And about appreciation of everything! The fact is that I am ONE and I recognize and accept this fact. By reaching this point and really just knowing it and being able to truly feel this oneness in my heart and soul allows me to know that my energy and vibrational field is higher than many others I know or have ever known.

Man, humans, as a species, has many vibrational levels. I believe since love is all about harmony, and harmony, by definition means to flow with everything, that those that exist in harmony with ONE, will "graduate" to a "place" with a higher vibrational frequency. This is because in the big picture and in the "organization" of all the universes, harmony and order of the most extreme are what makes it all so perfect. With the human species, with man, our entire history has been one of disharmony. Disharmony is not in line with the order of the universe.

By definition and by scientific fact, disharmony always leads to destruction of the systems in which it exists. If a jet engine is not in tune as it's cylinders revolve around a central axis, if it becomes eccentric, it loses harmony with it's system and it starts to vibrate and it eventually destroys itself. If your tires are not balanced and your car is not properly aligned, it eventually has destructive consequences. If man continues to destroy the very environment he lives in, it has destructive outcomes. As stated before in previous essays, man is the destructive force on this planet called Earth we are presently visiting within this cosmic experiment.

So again, by definition, that entity that is not in harmony with the larger system of which it is a part of, will eventually eliminate itself from this system so that harmony and balance can be restored to the larger system. Thus, those human beings among us who do not live with love and harmony in their hearts and souls do not vibrate at a higher level so they do not ascend to a higher place. They will remain at a place that vibrates at a similar frequency to which their frequency is equal to others.

With a radio, you hear the sounds because the radio waves from that tower to which you are listening are all on the same frequency. If there are competing frequencies you hear only static because no harmony exists. So, to make progress as human beings, those who vibrate at higher frequencies on similar or identical wavelengths tend to find each other and continue their soul progressions.

In a crowded room, why are we drawn to a single particular individual? It is the fact that the frequency is similar. Why do we fall in love? Why do we cherish certain people as life long friends? Energy frequencies are close to one another. Man as a species destroys everything he is in contact with. It has always been so and will always be so until the end of his "reign" on this planet. The planet will survive, man will not because man is not in harmony with the larger entity which is earth. And man has even taken his destructive ways beyond the planet into space. Space will not tolerate man's pollution of it with such puny little forces when compared to universal forces. Man is a mere gnat with zero power over anything, let alone a disruptive force in the galaxy in which he is temporarily residing at this brief moment.

Man is near the end. Everything that destroys is eventually destroyed itself. With man, as in most cases, the destroyer eventually overreaches and destroys himself. God has zero to do with the present circumstances on this minuscule planet. Man alone has created this huge mess we are living in and he will do himself in by his own means. We see examples of this all around us with the actions of individuals, businesses, governments, etc. Eventually they are eliminated as a direct result of actions they themselves have initiated and have acted upon. As I frequently state, the answers are all around us. When a person recognizes the ONE, the answers become very clear. God speaks to us every day and those vibrating at a higher frequency become more tuned in and act accordingly.

ESSAY 31:
The Soul of Man, Part Two

For me, I am attempting self-transcendence in my trying to reach a higher vibrational plane than that which I was born into. I am trying to go higher than most of those around me. However, this is my individual journey, as all others have theirs. It is right for me in my present level of consciousness. I am a "seeker" for I seeking ascendency on my eternal journey towards attainment. Of course, one can never reach that station. But I recognize that the journey itself is the attainment, not attainment itself. Thus, transcendence is the pathway one must follow on the journey to attainment, which can never be achieved.

Also, "individual" souls are not individual at all per se. For all souls are ONE as is everything ONE. However, there does exist a different vibration in all these souls that are part of the ONE. Similar to a igneous rock vibrating at a different level from a sedimentary rock. Just as there is a unique set of characteristics for each individual person, all these persons are human beings who belong to the family of man. Why aren't souls the same way? An innocent and unspoiled child is certainly different from a Koch brother!

With evolution, man has evolved from a creature of the sea to a mammal on land to eventually become the species of Homo Sapiens that he is at present. Thus, over millions of years, man has come to this point. He has evolved from a very primitive life form to what he is today. As stated before in other essays, all the answers to everything are all around us if we pay attention. Why is it so difficult to imagine that as man has evolved in his physical form he has not also evolved in his spiritual realm? Some argue that life has no meaning. It is all just an "accident" or a cosmic "joke". How could something so perfect, i.e. all systems on Earth, in our galaxy, in all the galaxies, in all the universes be an accident!!?? It is just so awesomely perfect!

So many people feel that what they do, how they think, how they behave makes absolutely no difference to anything. Yet any person with any sense at all comes to realize that all actions taken have consequences, eventually, to someone, even them. Animals know that if they are not vigilant, they will be consumed by another. They learn to be careful, or they die. They are aware of the consequences of a wrong choice. Thus the humans who live this way, at such primitive awareness, do not "get it". They do not increase their vibrational levels while here, thus they do not ascend. They repeat, they descend, or they cease to vibrate beyond a pebble of sand.

So as humans rise above their circumstances of birth, their environments, their hardships, their obstacles, and their suffering, they attain higher stations in life than from whence they began. They become more actualized and they reap the earthly benefits of the way they have lived and "invested" in their lives. So too, do those who strive to grow their spiritual awareness attain a higher vibration that propels them beyond many others. Again, this is not a competition, this is an individual spiritual growth process that is rewarded at a higher level.

Alike energy frequencies potentiate each other. A man fortunate enough to fall in love and marry a woman on a higher frequency such as he can soar in life! They both can! They fuse and they journey onward and upward into the heavens. I do believe this to be very rare. But vibrational frequencies, like higher radio frequencies, penetrate deeper into the universe and are more "creative" than lesser ones. This ascension continues through eternity.

These individuals have learned the GOD lesson of LOVE! Love of everything and appreciation and wonderment for all that GOD hath made and all the perfection thereof! They know what it means to grasp the concept of ONE. They realize that they are compelled to live a life of meaning. Phycholigists tell us that many more people chose death by suicide because they feel their life has no meaning than because they do not feel they are loved. Many people know they are loved, they write letters of apology to their loved ones, yet they choose to die by suicide! Thus to them, their life had no meaning!

One's life has to have value to that person, or it loses meaning. It follows then that the creation and existence of man must also have meaning, for why would God create man if it were to have no meaning?! The meaning must be to live in love and harmony and appreciation with all life forms, animal, vegetable, and mineral. And to be so very, very thankful and grateful for this divine gift of life!

God granted man freedom in that he is free to make personal choices about everything. He has a developed mind, an awareness, a consciousness. But, man must also learn that those free choices all have consequences, to oneself and to others. Those that learn to live in this manner vibrate higher. Those who do not learn or do severe harm or do not believe in anything higher than themselves are destined to be weeded out for they are destructive to the harmony of the universe. They become but a grain of sand, or less.

ESSAY 32:

Defending Excellence... NE Patriots, UCONN Women

I dare to present the NE Patriots football team and the UCONN women basketball teams, among others, as examples of sustained excellence. What is not to be admired and applauded when these teams have continued to dominate their sport for such a long time? Only persons who are aware of how difficult this is to achieve can truly appreciate all the effort and sacrifice that is necessary for this to happen. These teams are so rare and so beautiful to observe that it is a joy to watch them dominate their foes time after time. They have proven themselves so many times that there is an expectation and a confidence they display that is so instructional on how to live an examined life. Just knowing there is always a way and a price, but confident in your abilities to be successful again and again.

Truly a lesson to all of us who just need to look and study the habits of accomplished people to realize anyone who truly wants to, can. No matter what the want, the can do attitude is within that individual. Look at Aaron Rogers, as I have alluded to before. To watch his mastery of his chosen craft, his calmness, his resolve, his performance, his decision making, his choreography, is to watch perfection, art, and absolute confidence in his abilities. What is not beautiful about watching anybody be so flawless as he does his thing?

Tom Brady also. Sheer total command of his environment. He has winner written all over him. And not just football, but everything he chooses to focus on. He pays the price also. He puts in the time, eats, sleeps, studies, practices, all the things that the average person does not "want" to do. They feel their effort is enough to get by as best they can and no need to push much harder to gain more. They have "enough" for the effort they are willing to expend.

They have no desire to push themselves beyond their comfort zone. To me, rather than being safe, I feel comfort zones are frequently dangerous places. They can become growth and development and spirit killers. Just depends on what a person wants from life. Comfort is overrated and insidious. Too much comfort begets the desire for more comfort, and that can be a person's downfall as a spiritual exercise in living. Entropy can set in and downhill results from that. Mind, body, and spirit start their decline and the earlier one becomes too comfortable, the quicker the process accelerates.

See it everywhere. People of certain wealth just want more and they often lose their values and their health. Their lives become devoid of meaning or value. Boredom ensues, thus they have affairs, drugs and alcohol, workaholics, etc. and all lead them downward. So, when I watch people who live with passion in their lives, I observe and appreciate their spirits. They excel at something that, to them, means something special and they are enthusiastic and savor their times of production and contribution to whatever they are doing. These people tend to be much happier, excited, hard working (but not really work to them), enthusiastic, content, but not in a "mission accomplished" mindset. Usually they have many friends because people enjoy being in the presence of their uplifting energy. They tend to feel confident and good about themselves and that radiates into their personal relationships with others. They live happy lives of fulfillment and satisfaction.

ESSAY 33:

TRUE LOVE...What I perceive love to be.

I know this is rare, to experience true love. This is what I believe love to be. There is initially a strong physical attraction, physiological also. There must be passion between both parties. Love making would be intense and physically and emotionally and spiritually fulfilling on all levels. It is not a duty, but a shared joy much enjoyed by both parties. There must be mutual respect, admiration, and pride in one another. Love is never selfish. You would both want the other to be their own person. Each must be secure in who they are. You share your lives and most experiences, but you have the freedom to freely express your individual needs also. No assigned blame, guilt or shame.

You should be similar in your values and in your mutual interests. However, each should feel free to get their individual needs and interests satisfied independent of the other. There should be no price to pay for these differences. Healthy couples are actively supportive and proud of the accomplishments of the other. You should be true partners in your mutual life journey together. You should feel safe and secure enough to share everything going on in your life with your mate. You should be willing to suffer together. Your partner's pain is your pain. You should always be there for each other. You should celebrate the accomplishments of the other as if they were your own.

You should not expect to be "taken care of" by your partner. Each should be willing to carry his own weight. Each has different skills and they should work together using each one's strengths to elevate them both as they navigate through life. They should both devote themselves to growth and development and support the efforts of the other to this end. They should truly appreciate having the other intimately in their life. They should really enjoy being in the other's company, yet give each other the space they need when they need it. Each should be truly interested in what the other is doing. Encourage one another.

Be able to look in the eyes of the other and feel the love being reciprocally returned back to them. Have a similar sense of humor. Be willing to roll up your sleeves when needed. Always be willing to do more than your share. Do not be jealous, envious nor resentful. Be able to have fun together. Be able to have long and deep talks with one another.

ESSAY 34:
Bigger than you

How does one deal with life? Everything that happens to us as humans is bigger than you. Until/unless we learn to accept this fact, we will always be lost. Lost souls. That is our choice! We could ask, what is the message for me at this time? What is my big picture? What can this teach me? How do I grow from this? How do I identify and retain my God given power? If I appear to "lose" in human terms, how do I ultimately win and depart with a satisfied smile on my face? I fought the gallant battle. I kept my personal integrity, my honor, my dignity till the end. I did the very best I could with the hand I was dealt. So how is that a "loss"? That is a true win on all spiritual levels! That is living your divinity! One's spiritual entity is all that remains permanent, throughout eternity. The continuum goes on, forever.

God is speaking to me as I write these words.. I am not actually hearing voices. Rather, these thoughts are arising from deep within me. He has done this with me for many years. I have always taken pause and listened. I just feel His presence, His wisdom, His guidance at my deepest core. We all, each and every one of us, possess this deep core. It is up to each of us to learn to slow down, venture within, listen, feel, observe and have total trust in His plan for us. This must be done individually and as a species. However, we can only be responsible for ourselves as individuals. The human race must get the message collectively or it will eliminate itself soon enough.

ESSAY 35:
Age 77, my latest and newest adventure

As I have written before, my life is assigned and very briefly loaned to me. All the events of this life have been directed by God. He gave me my experiences, my observations, my learnings, my values, my beliefs. To my credit, I have always accepted where I was on this life journey. I have never played the victim role. I have just trusted in Him and moved forward, always forward. This has given me strength and purpose in my life. I have no choice but to continue to follow His lead for me. To counter all that I am, would be to negate my entire life.

Thus, here I am, at age 77 now. I am not tired but I am weary. I am frustrated by the ignorance in the human race. I am fortunate that I can still see that I have talents and desires that can continue to help my fellow man. I can still improve the lives of those around me. I can soothe their pains and improve their self-esteem and quality of life, and make their lives better. How selfish I would be to only think of myself and "relaxation and vegetation" as the way to end my life. I have always lived fully in the arena of life and to abandon that way of living near my end would be an act of killing myself. I have never lived on the sidelines of life. Never! And I refuse to change my beliefs and compromise my integrity as a human being with the life code and principles I have had my entire life on this planet!

I am so fortunate and blessed that I have received, perceived and accepted this divine message since childhood. I have always sensed this fleeting impermanence of life and the calling to make my life matter to others. Truly attempt to make a dedicated effort to make a positive difference!

I simply must continue to do everything in my power to be of comfort and service to those who just need my unique help. This is professional and specific help that I have developed the skills and knowledge over a lifetime to learn and implement and practice. I realize that my skills in this dental community are sorely needed. I can still offer all that I can to these people. My overall knowledge, experience, empathy, communication skills, demeanor, and comforting manner are still of value. I can still do my part.

...NOTE TO READERS....These words were originally written and intended for my eyes only, to myself. I was trying to get pumped up to convince myself I could still do it. Not intended to appear puffed up to others. No way. I composed this as I was trying to decide if I should open up a new dental practice in my deep golden years.

I feel there is no choice for me at this late stage in my life. For me, to be truly alive is to continually strive to to live a life of meaning, as long as reasonably possible. God will tell me when it is time to back off. I do not feel any such thing as yet. I pray I can find a younger version of myself to continue my work when my time is over. Again, God will provide my answers. I am not attached. I accept what will be. I trust.

ESSAY 36:
Spiritual Awareness

What is spiritual awareness and why is it important? I realized many years ago that I have been truly blessed since childhood. I did not know this as I was growing up. I became conscious of being more sensitive to certain circumstances and events in life as I grew into adulthood than my peers and others older than me appeared to be. I just seemed to notice things and write about them from an early age. I especially did this when adversity came my way. By writing about the current turmoil, I could empty it from my active mind and be better able to remove myself mentally from what was happening.

By distancing myself, I could become separate from the problem. Thus, I was able to be more objective and learned to be more patient. By practicing patience from afar, I could become less attached to a specific outcome. Also, by trying to re-frame the event by not asking "what am I going to do about this", to "what can a person do who finds himself in this situation" I have discovered it can make a huge difference in how quickly the predicament is resolved. You have removed your emotions and your attachment to a particular preconceived desired result. That opens your mind for more possibilities.

For me, my answer would eventually come. The path to be taken would flow into my consciousness and then I could take action. In my life, it always has proven to be the correct action, even if the outcome appeared to have not been the initial desired one. Time revealed the correctness of the outcome. Sometimes it may take years to reveal the correctness. Time can be your friend. But, as I state frequently, you must pay attention!

So by withdrawing from the external problem and learning to go inward for the solution, you are developing your own Spiritual Awareness. You are learning patience, trust, surrender and acceptance, to whatever the end result of the current dilemma may be. As you practice this in your life, you grow yourself. You are evolving in that you are becoming more comfortable within yourself. You are connecting. You are becoming more relaxed, serene, more confident, more in control of what is going on inside you. You cannot control much that is external in your life. Life just happens. But you can learn to have total command of what goes on within you, internally.

As your spiritual awareness develops, you are granting yourself wonderful and lasting gifts. You become more centered, more connected to your true self, thus you are more connected to all that is. And by being connected to yourself at that deep spiritual level, you come to realize you are one with God, because He has always known your true self. You are now with God and you come to know this and feel this eternal connection with being ONE. You can feel this at your core. You just KNOW! Your life purpose will be discovered and celebrated by you. By knowing yourself intimately from deep within, you can better live your life with more meaning and passion. You will come to serenity, to internal peace, and quit chasing your tail on the treadmill of life as it exists in our external society today.

Life is such a fascinating experience when you learn to go within. The good and the bad can be mesmerizing. Unfortunately, one would correctly think on the surface, some of these events may be framed as horrific. And many are. But, eventually if you do your work, you may come to realize that sickness, severe hardship, loss, even tragedy are actually opportunities that should grab your attention and force you to go much deeper to make some sense of it all.

Actually you may never make sense of it in your lifetime. However, you have a golden opportunity to grow quantums at the spiritual level. But that is, of necessity, entirely up to you. If these severe events cannot force you to go deep inside and get in intimate touch with your spirit, you may never be able to reach the level of spiritual awareness each human being is capable of.

What is really important in life will become more apparent to you as your awareness and connection within yourself grows. Obstacles and setbacks will be dealt with more easily and effectively. Some attachments will become stronger and some will simply fade away. Outcomes will be more readily accepted for what they are. You adjust, you reframe, you move forward. Always strive to move forward but appreciate where you are in the present moment.

When you grasp the concept of being spiritually aware, you will gain your personal power and soar in life in all that truly matters. And what really matters will become so very apparent to you. You will be ready to meet your Maker when He calls you. And you will thank Him for the wonderful gift of life He granted you. You will have done your work and God will be so pleased and happy for you. For by living your truth, at the deepest level, you have lived God's truth, for He granted you that truth at your birth. Mission accomplished! Onward! Next!

ESSAY 37:
Millionnaire

What would I do with a couple million dollars socked away in the market? First and foremost, it did not flow that way for me. If I was making money in the market, I would be watching it every single day. Should I hold, buy, or sell? Gotta watch it, every single day. Be concerned or be joyful or be worried? The more I made, the more I would want to make. How much should I take out, and when? Where should I put it that is "safe" and gets a decent return? Should I buy some houses in different places and travel there on a schedule to keep tabs on them? Always keeping track of upkeep, taxes, fees, overhead, repairs, insurance, etc. Thus, just another thing to take care of and watch over. A stealer of time and of life.

Thus, in that way, money does not free you as much as it places more burdens upon you. More to worry about, more to watch over, more to "protect". Constantly contemplating what you should purchase next for you can now better "afford" it. So, you start failing to really see the truth and wisdom behind having just about or "enough", rather than having the need for always more. Money is a strange thing. It is so insidious how it changes one's thinking. To an aware person, as they age and become reflective of their lives, people were the happiest when they had less but yet just enough to get by.

The early struggles and challenges were initially exciting and invigorating and stimulating. We had no choice. We were trying to just survive and lay the foundation for our future together. They made one happy to be alive and we appreciated the simplicity, the things that truly mattered. Everything was in the moment. I remember when I was working as a waiter at a higher end restaurant at night when I was in dental school. My wife and I were beyond broke. I would take any left-over uneaten steak or portions of meals or whatever home and we would have a feast! Food never tasted better!

When one starts to get some money, things usually change. What money can buy can become a quest that may become addictive in that "MORE" is seen as better and MORE never ends for far too many people. The disease of "MORE" is insidious and it can kill you in so many ways. So, I feel fortunate in that having the desire for trying to have more money just so I have "security" became of no meaning to me. I know the trap. Security is an illusion and to devote so much time and energy to attaining wealth in the belief that wealth begets security is so foolish in my eyes.

For me, just to live simply with the basics plus a few perks is more than OK. I much prefer this mind-set vs. wasting my days, weeks, months, and years in the pursuit of wealth. I want to have just enough to do some (not all) of the things that are important to me. I have so much less to watch over and I can better appreciate the things I do have.

It seems to me that people who have personal insecurities or self-worth issues tend to need to insulate and prop themselves up with the "security" and image generated by having some degree of wealth. These people seem to need to validate and prove to others, strangers even, that because they have money, they are special, gifted, chosen, desirable winners. Don't you love me, admire me, envy me, want to be me? They need this external validation for they are internally empty on some level. I am fortunate because I can see the futility of such a quest. I feel very centered in who I am and what my values are. I feel I have done the work necessary to reach this awareness that I have as it pertains to me. I can only speak to me and for me.

So, my attitude about money is liberating to me. It frees me up to think about more important things than accumulating scraps of paper in exchange for more "things". It measures zero about a person. It elevates no-one above what their character and values demonstrate them to be. It is pure folly to spend time and effort accumulating more than you need. Better to spend that time on something of lasting value.

Values clarification is something that too few people spend the time and effort doing. They are too busy chasing whatever, to even be aware of the true lessons and simple rewards of living one's life in a more simple and truly meaningful way. Sadly, most have no clue as to what meaning is. It is just so difficult for them to get off that treadmill. Many people know that to evaluate the health of your heart, the Doctor may order a stress test on a treadmill. And many people die on that treadmill.

ESSAY 38:

Suggestions on How to "Figure it Out"

We had a lake cabin in Western South Dakota. We spent years there with our young children on summer week-ends. After everyone was in bed, I would remove myself and lounge on our deck. There was zero ambient light. No streetlights, no traffic, no noise, no floodlights or yard lights. SD is a rather flat state. On a moonless night, you could see an endless planetarium in the night sky. Actually, it was beyond seeing it. It was experiencing it. It was connecting with it. It was becoming ONE with it!

I could see the Milky Way in vivid detail. The constellations, the space station, satellites. Meteor showers were like fireworks.I would sit and watch for hours. It was such an overwhelming experience in so many ways. My elderly father visited one time from New Jersey. We were sitting there together on the deck. He looked up and remarked in childhood amazement that he had not seen such a sky in decades! He had forgotten that so many stars existed! City lights hide such wonders.

I made this a common practice. To create the moments when I could just sit in solitude and contemplate all that is. And was. And shall ever be. The sheer vastness. The order. The design. The perfection. I came to the recognition of how small we human beings actually are in the "Big Picture". Looking at that endless and vast night sky is beyond humbling. And that view is humongous! We are nothing! Why do we spend so much time and energy believing that what we do in our brief lives makes any difference to anything? Why do we think everything revolves around us? Why are we so into our egos that we believe we really matter? Why is it all about us? Why do we believe we are so important, so "unique" and special?

Of course, I have concluded we are not important in a physical sense. We are so temporary. But we are very important in a spiritual sense. And our spirits are permanent, just as the universe is permanent. An analogy I can offer is about the ocean and it's surface vs. beneath the surface. When a severe storm is occurring, it is totally on the surface. The waves can range from ten feet to 100 feet and beyond! There is danger, turbulence, chaos on the surface. However, beneath the surface all is calm. Nothing deep beneath is being threatened or disturbed . All is well there. So it is with the external physical and the deeper internal spiritual.

When one recognizes how puny and temporary and insignificant our physical existence is and understands that deep beneath our physical surface exists a serenity and calmness that can never exist on the external surface, we can come to realize the "answer". The answer is: we must redirect our focus from outside to inside. We must seek to abandon our egos and learn to become ONE with all that is. We must strive to connect to the universal energy that is forever. This energy is within all of us. Doing so will relieve us of all our meaningless attachments to things that have no lasting value. Then, we ascend to the stars and beyond and become all we can be. There we find our true peace, on Earth as it is in Heaven. With God's guidance and blessing!

ESSAY 39:
Hands, an Appreciation

Being a dentist, obviously hands are crucial to me. As they are, of course, to all human beings. I suspect most of us do not think one second about hands, unless we are to suffer the misfortune of losing one or both. So, I choose to share my thoughts on the entire idea of hands.

HANDS... Hands speak of effort, service, toil, experiences, adventures, hardship and suffering, strength, weakness, pleasures, skills, maturation, and state of health. In darkness, one's hands provide us with a means to see. They allow us to pray, to feel, to nurture and comfort, to sustain ourselves with food and drink. They make it possible for us to do work, to make love, to explore and discover, to play, to perceive, to entertain, amuse and speak. We use them to communicate, better express ourselves, to learn, to greet and to say goodbye.

They alert us to danger, to our environment, weather, temperature and sensations. For many, a sunset, flowers, animals, and nature, can give flight to the soul. So too, can music and music is only made possible with our hands. In such a way, hands can also free our soul. Thus hands, in short, enhance our lives in ways in which our essence as human beings is made possible.

Hands are a powerful testimonial to the evolution of man. They are a marvel of engineering with an opposing thumb that makes being totally human possible. Hands facilitate the myriad of human experiences. They speak to who we are. They tell a marvelous story about all that we are and the summation of all we have experienced in our life, thus creating memories. The story they tell can become truly spiritual, in their own special way.

They are the silent narrative of our life. Thus, by taking the time to really observe them, to explore and study them, we bear witness to the power of what they have to say. They can evoke feelings of power, wisdom, strength, love, forgiveness, perseverance, acceptance, comfort, patience, and tolerance. By taking a long moment from time to time, you may reach a new appreciation for something many of us just take for granted.

ESSAY 40:
Effort and Success...
A Question

A philosophical question..... Is it better to put out 50% effort and succeed or put out 100% effort and fail? I feel it is better to put out total effort, for in doing so one learns what that feels like and it becomes a habit. Thus, throughout life, you will do better in all areas. That is why "B and C" students find so much more satisfaction and overall success. They learn to work harder and smarter. People who do well with minimum effort find it ultimately catches up with them.

Outstanding natural athletes when young do not put in the practice time to get better. It is so easy for them they never bother. As they grow older, they find the average athletes are passing them by. They do this because they are more driven and more hungry and more willing to do the extra things to be all they are capable of being. When their playing days are over, they make better coaches than the natural athlete because how can a natural teach to others less gifted what is second nature for them?

If one achieves success with little effort, they believe they will always be successful in whatever they attempt. Thus, they can over-reach and lose it all with no tools to recover. They can also feel like imposters and know it was all luck and then self-destruct with guilt like I believe Freddy Prinze did. My opinion is success was just all just too easy and too early for him and he did not feel he had earned it. Certainly not more deserving than people he believed to be more talented who paid their dues over many years and just never caught the big break that he did.

Also, undeserving successful people can tend to get a very "puffed up" and arrogant attitude. They feel superior to those who have not been fortunate enough to reach their station in life. They expect deference and homage and often lack empathy. They make demands and have expectations because of who they are. They do not accept responsibility.

ESSAY 41:
Diminishing Yourself

Never diminish yourself to anyone, especially to a perceived lessor person. To permit this is to give your power to them. Never give your power to another, unless you need to do so, temporarily, in order to better serve your future needs at that point in time. Bide your time. Develop a plan. Be prepared to act. When the flow reveals itself, act. Now is the time to assert your power, when you are in a better position to do so. It is time to meet your needs not theirs.

Be patient and play the hand you were dealt. In recognizing this fact, one can still retain his power and use it when necessary to get his needs met without being victimized in any way. Do not permit this and you retain your power over the situation. Oftentimes one must withdraw for a time. This backing off is not a weakness, although it may be perceived as such by your adversary. It is strength, your strength over your situation. Just a pause as you figure your way out of this circumstance. Yield to no one if it means diminishing yourself. There is a cost when you ultimately surrender to the demands of you by another to serve their needs of you vs. your needs of you. To grow yourself, you must believe in yourself.

ESSAY 42:
Hubbub and noise

In my present situation, one of good fortune and gratitude, I am looking out over the ocean from 9 stories up. I am feeling such gratitude for life. Had I had lots of money or fame, I would be so consumed with so many worries, concerns, and distractions that I would not be available in my mind to really see and appreciate all the glory of God's wonder. So, I am feeling truly blessed. I am an observer and an involved and active participant in my own God- given life and I so appreciate this opportunity I have. I take nothing for granted-ever. Thank you my dear God!

ESSAY 43:
The Gift of Need

When one is lacking something that he really needs, he truly appreciates that need. As such, he is so much more aware and conscious of everything around him. When a bit hungry, he truly enjoys and savors food, more than ever. Thirst also. Taking a trip when it has been far too long since the previous one, really is so much more satisfying than simply knowing you can always do as you please whenever. When you really feel you need something vs. you want something, you are truly living in the moment. All your focus is concentrated on meeting that need.

When you are in need, you shed the cloak of complacency and boredom and the entropy of having everything, and feeling "satisfied". With having "it all" you may come to realize, or not, that such conditions can become insidious and subtle robbers of a meaningful and fully lived and appreciated life. The gift is taken for granted and one is lulled into a sense of entitlement, privilege, pomposity, and false sense of self-worth.

Empathy for others becomes lacking as you begin to judge and look down on those less fortunate. You tend to become judgmental and assign blame to these persons who find themselves in situations of hardship. You justify not lending a hand, for it becomes "their fault" they find themselves in this situation. If they were as smart as you, they would not be in this situation, is your excuse. You may find some satisfaction in this for it elevates you and diminishes them, in your eyes. These are the actions and thoughts of very small people, unevolved and self-centered and selfish.

Having simple needs stimulates your senses and every single moment is felt much more acutely and not taken for granted. One is more alert and thus truly feels his life and the minute events in it more acutely. One truly is living in the present, for he is aware that moment is very precious and can never be taken for granted. Living with need is truly living totally in the NOW, for the future is recognized as uncertain.

ESSAY 44:

Birds...The Lessons right before me

As I sit here watching these birds in the cold and harsh winter, I see the necessary struggle for survival. These creatures of God do not ever get to "retire." They do not sit around taking it easy and have all their needs taken care of by others. Every single day, no matter what the weather or how they are feeling, they must go out and "earn a living", or they die, period! Work or die, very simple. Only with humans, do we expect to be taken care of by the "system." Yet, we humans complain how unfair life is. How it should now be easier or simpler.

Why should we be exempt from the laws of nature that all other life creatures must abide by to survive yet another day? You work, you rest, and you, with the grace of God, live another day. That is the contract of life. Accept that fact and life is as it is meant to be and as good as it is supposed to be. Deny or reject that premise and you suffer the difficult consequences of your choice of the "easy" path. Again, how do you choose to frame the circumstances of your life?

I am alive. I am in decent health, hopefully. Does one lament certain circumstances they may be in and have a pity party? No! This is life, good and not so good. Struggles and obstacles hopefully followed by victories and satisfaction. Ups and downs. Pluses and minuses. In our case, we have, at times in the past, found ourselves in the circumstance of paying backward, rather than forward. We had "compromised" our possible future for the certainty of living in our today, rather than postponing today so we may be able to hopefully live ahead, somewhere, sometime down the road, in a not guaranteed future. Maybe!

We could have chosen not to do all the things we have done all those years past and saved more money and thus had the finances available to finally start doing what we had already done and have been doing. I would rather have the certainty and the enjoyment and the learnings of those travels taken and experiences and friendships formed, than to just be beginning at the age of 70! How in the world can you gain those 30 years when you just begin at 70!? I am feeling like tapering off rather than just beginning!

Why would I ever want to trade with those who may have more financial security, yet delayed starting to create priceless moments until they retire? You can possibly make more money but you cannot make more time! What is the point of living a life such as this? How aware and developed and tested and spiritual can such a life be? To me, that life is so void and un-lived. To each his own. Choices. I choose to keep my own wheelbarrow of stones, thank you. We "played" as we could along the way, now we pay a little bit more. That was our bargain with life. Yet another test. Simple, clear-cut and correct, on a spiritual level. Law of Nature. Basic.

A vast majority of people do not enjoy what they are doing to earn a living. It truly is work for them. But, look at many actors, legislators, congressmen, Warren Buffet types, professionals, Albert Sweitzer, Supreme Court Justices, etc. Even the Queen. They all worked until they could no longer do so. They do this because they love what they do. It is an integral part of their identity, who they are. Some of them have lived out of balance lives. All they did was work. For me, there must be a work-play balance. This balance facilitates my staying involved in life in a growth-producing and stimulating and healthy way.

Many of those who retire early usually do so because they have made enough money and they just want to "play" now. They postponed, but they often discover they needed to learn the lesson that too much leisure teaches. More frequently, they hated their jobs and could not wait to get out. And then to do what, for many have no clue what to do with all that structureless free time. These people have lessons to learn also. We all have our times and circumstances presented to us to learn our lessons, but how few take advantage of this spiritual opportunity? As I state many times, we are all on different paths. Who is to say which is right or wrong? If it is right for you, and it does no harm to others, it is right. Period!

ESSAY 45:
Arriving "Home" to a Serene Environment, in my LIfe

I perceive myself, rightly or wrongly, to be a bit different than many people in lots of ways. I realize I have more than enough severe blind spots in some areas but I do believe I have some gifts and very clear vision, to me, that I feel very blessed to be aware of in this lifetime. I am who I am and I have taken some risks and I have made some mistakes. Such is life in the arena. No person since I reached adulthood, no employer or government entity has ever taken care of me and as a result, in my opinion, left me handicapped and puffed up by being untested, yet believing I was omnipotent or entitled.

Over the last six years in our retirement we have maintained 3 residences and traveled extensively. It eventually proved to be too exhausting and harried. Just too much to take care of and maintain. It was very expensive also and we had to get out of it and slow ourselves down. We have now rid ourselves of all the maintaining "of places" and traveling logistics and headaches. Thus, we have now "done that" and are currently navigating ourselves to another new adventure. We have simplified greatly.

We have satisfied the travel bug these last 25 years and made life-long friends and memories in the process. Priceless and comforting reminiscences in our now upon us, golden years. Very satisfying years well lived. We just want simple now. We are now centered in Vermont, where life is not as hectic and complicated. We control the pace. It is a nice fit for us. No social pressures, yet with congruent values with this unique and special state. We are very comfortable in this tranquil and uncomplicated environment and all its splendor in a nature abundant setting. Healthy food and lifestyle. Good values based on plain common sense and decency. Vermont truly is a "State of Mind".

We are "coming home" to where it all began; lakes, mountains, streams, winding country roads, foliage, rainy and snowy days. Our ancestors all came from this heritage, in England, Ireland and Scotland (Germany too). This is our natural circadian rhythm. We are truly where we belong. We feel peace here. It is correct for me. I am provided precious solitude when I desire and need it. My wife, Bonnie, has friends and family (seventh generation Vermonter!) so she feels connected and safe. We each can have our own time, together and apart. This is healthy and necessary for growth.

As I age, I desire more time to think, remember, process, reflect and relax. To loosely make plans too, when needed. I am feeling comfortable, satisfied, and content where I find myself now. Serenity lives here for me. Challenges are different now in some ways, but I find little stress because I have been in stressful situations and environments so many times before in my life. This is familiar territory for me and I feel confident I can transform any "bumps" into another positive growth opportunity and learning experience. The challenges in life and our responses to them are so affirming to the state of being truly alive! Be an active participant in your own life! How blessed are those who attempt to live as truly alive, really are! It is up to each of us to be fully engaged in this wondrous gift from God. Thank you God! Amen.

ESSAY 46:
Connecting with the DIVINE

How does one connect with the Divine spirit within each of us? We each must seek our own methods. For me, I attempt to create an environment, in solitude, where I can carve out an hour or so just for myself. I am seeking to be "exported" or "transported" to that sacred place, deep within me. It can be walking barefoot on a beach, at sunrise or sunset. Listening to music and immersing myself in it. Closing my eyes while sitting reclined or lying down facing the sun. I am feeling it, absorbing it's nurturing and caressing energy and I am seeing bright red colors beneath my eyelids that seem to be dancing and darting about.

It can be so many things to each of us. Looking up at the vast Milky Way on a clear moonless night and just staring at the stars and feeling the connection. Sitting by a babbling brook and absorbing the rhythmic sounds. Become ONE with those sounds. Listening to rain on a tin roof. Exercising long enough to get an endorphin high. Swimming at a relaxed steady pace and becoming ONE with the caressing water. Kayaking a mountain lake at dawn or dusk. Fishing in a stream or in solitude. Snow skiing on fresh fallen snow or while heavy snow is falling.

Water skiing on water smooth as glass under a full moon. When I did this, my first born 12 year old daughter was driving the boat. I could feel my deep connection with being ONE with the water beneath my feet and the generation after me and the moon in the heavens up above and with all the generations that preceded mine. It was such an extreme emotional rush that I was laughing and crying with pure joy at the same time! Unreal existential experience!! The circle of life that never ends!

For some who have developed a rather deep outer crust to shield us from the assaults of life, it can be a bit helpful to peel that rougher outer skin of the onion back a layer. At times I find that having a beer or glass of wine, can be just enough to mellow me out so I can let my guard down. My objective is to be relaxed a tiny bit so as to be better able to open the gates ever so slightly, to facilitate communication and connection more easily. I want to be receptive to enlightening myself, not to escape from myself. Thus, do nothing more than is required for you to get to that very special place. Just put your toe in, do not submerge yourself.

The goal is for each of us to ID our own unique spiritual places or activities. Opportunities where we can feel our true connection to that force that created us. You will come to seek these places out more frequently, for as you go deeper within and get more familiar with your true self, you will discover your answers will come more frequently and more easily. Your awareness will deepen and you will become more patient and accepting of yourself. Life will become easier, even if outside events remain difficult and tumultuous.

ESSAY 47:
Getting back in the Moment

When I tend to get somewhat down, as we all do at certain times, I realize it is a natural cycle for everyone and try to cut myself some slack. Be patient, give yourself some time and space. When you feel you may be ready, try to change your setting or routine or get physically active. I need to remind myself that to stay down too long solves nothing. It robs me of the moment I am missing by my depressed state. I must always strive to conquer this. I am robbing myself of the now for the future, which is not even guaranteed. How dumb is that?!

ESSAY 48:

Fear!!!

FEAR!!! Wow, so many people allow fear to rule and control their lives! Governments, employers, spouses, family, religions, experts, insurance companies, etc. They ALL use fear to control and manipulate others to meet their agendas, not yours, IF you even do have an agenda! They will tell you "You must not worry, for they will provide an agenda for you", albeit with your permission (read, surrender). A person who is evolving into an examined (read tested, introspective) life, must NEVER allow fear to rule over them! It is NEVER as bad as they would lead you to believe. NEVER! And what is the ultimate fear? That one will die!? So, accept that fact and embrace it and be at peace with it and you will be more than OK with what tests God dials up for you, and HE WILL!!

That is the game and that is the challenge and that is what one signs up for when one emerges from that safe and secure womb. From that moment forward, within reason till we become old enough, "safe and secure" becomes the "objective" for each of us, our individual challenge and responsibility. The free ride is over.

We are now on our own, with only GOD to truly guide us. So, an astute individual, a survivor, an evolving person, will accept the bargain that was struck with God at his conception. I grant you the supreme and divine GIFT of life and you accept this gift on the terms that EVERY test I place upon you, you accept and do not curse. You confront this latest challenge, you do not succumb to fear or doubt.

Rather, you say to GOD that you will honor HIM by proving you are strong enough to give all you are capable of, to be up to this task HE has laid before you.

You have the faith to know that HE will protect you as long as you do everything in your power to overcome this obstacle. If the outcome is not ideal, and yet you have given all you can to combat this circumstance you are in, God will protect you, even if it means HE will release you and lead you home again. HE will honor and reward your supreme effort. That too, is a gift. You have surrendered, after giving your all, trying your very best. You did not curse God. You thank God for all the good things you have been privileged to experience with HIS grace while you were briefly visiting this planet called Earth.

I truly believe that the people who challenge, who take risks, who dream, who strive, who think, who engage life; they are the ones who truly grasp the true essence of what it is like to be truly alive. They do not always choose the "safe and secure" path. They are skeptics. They do take calculated risks that people seeking "security" do not take. "Secure" people tend to frequently look down on the risk takers. We are perceived as foolish. We are on a totally different wavelength. "Secure" people just do not get it, that security is whimsical. It can all change in seconds. When it is all taken away, ie. their lifetime of postponed pleasures and delayed gratification, only then do they just begin to see the folly of their ways. But then, it is over, too late. They are lost, they have no tools, their quills are out of arrows.

Persons such as I, will make our own arrows and continue the hunt, blessed and appreciative of all the previous tests we have overcome and knowing that this too, shall pass. A friend of ours did it all "right". He provided for his five children and his wife. He worked until the day he died at age 71. He NEVER had any of the travel experiences we have enjoyed for over 25 years! And we were still younger than he was when he died! Yes, he had some wealth but what was the point? What was the point?!

The point is that he made, in my mind, unselfish, yet unwise choices. He gave his entire life in service to his large family and not one of them had any true appreciation for all his years of sacrifice, toil, and efforts. He was taken for granted, wife included. She never worked outside the home, even after the children were raised. And she still lives as a pampered matriarch Queen on the fruits of his labors. This dear man did NOT live an examined life! He surrendered because it was the "normal and accepted and conventional" path. He did all the "correct" things and "lived" the "American Dream". It killed him, for what?!

Thus, if those who think and believe as I, are perceived as not "secure", in reality, we actually are. Because we have figured out our "rules" along the way. We know the game and we know the true winners and losers. Of course, I have made many mistakes, yet who has not? We are all human beings. What do we do about these mistakes? That is a test. We all have our tests, burdens, obstacles.

That is how it has to be and should be. Others have passed their tests and I will continue to pass mine, with the grace of God. Why would not God test me and why would I not strive to meet HIS test? HE would not test me if HE did not believe I could meet the test. Thus, it truly is up to me, for it is my test. I feel fortunate that I have had many tests and each new one becomes the current one. So, I have another opportunity to grow and that is a good thing. Growth sustains life!! It does not end it. So, I fear not. Rather, I trust in my GOD!!

ADVERSITY........ I do not seek it, nor do I reject it. The human spirit can overcome most anything. But, the will must be there. The strong can not only survive, they can thrive. Re: California Chrome race horse. They were offered millions of dollars to sell this horse before the Kentucky Derby. They stated that when you sell your dream, you sell your soul. No sale for ANY price! I agree 1000%! There are things you just do not do! Only a person who dreams and ventures forward accepting risk can possibly understand that concept.

Security minded people do not have a clue what a purposeful life means. Everything has a price for them and everything is for sale at the right price, in their pitiful little empty world. Shells of human beings in my opinion. Shells are everywhere, especially among many of the rich and famous. Nothing inside them at all that matters. Just passing through and building empty monuments to themselves that zero people care about except they themselves.

Think the Carnegies, Rockerfellers, Mellons, etc. They unmercifully squash the little guys on their way to great power and wealth and they then give a little away on their deathbeds to "benefit" humanity. Thus, they have perceived clear consciences when they meet their Maker. But, the Maker knows and so do the perpetrators, on some level. If they do not, they are totally bankrupt humanoids, not even human beings, in God's image. It is all about image and perception. The doer of deeds knows his true intent and so does our Maker.

ESSAY 49:
Existential Question, "Charity"

If a person is always helping others or giving valued possessions away, does the motive matter? Is it because they need to do this in order to feel better about themselves? Is that a valid reason, for then it is about them and not the recipient? What if they just feel such joy and a sense of well- being in giving to others. Is that not also a selfish reason, for it makes them feel to be more worthy human beings? Not as much, I would believe. The thing is, everything a human being does, is done for a selfish reason on some level. If a deserving person needs help and I know this and I can help but choose to not do so, do I not suffer some guilt? Of course I do. Thus, by helping out I am serving myself also, for I am not going to be eaten up with guilt. Thus my helping could be perceived as a selfish act.

Also, consider a rich person who gives away a lot of money, yet has so much he will never miss it. Then a poor person gives part of what he has and it makes a real serious dent in his finances. Who is the better person? Who is really the rich one, the one more God-like? The rich donate because they have it to give, they gain public accolades, a tax write-off, and they may feel some guilt. Or, like so many of that ilk, they feel they "earned" it and so "let the "unfortunates" be on their own and help themselves." The rich often feel more entitled than fortunate.

ESSAY 50:

Where you are is Here, Now...Appreciation and Acceptance

NOTE...I need to remind readers that these essays were written by me, for me and my children. They were a journal of my own private thoughts as I am aging. The decision to publish came much later. Thus, there is no intention to put ego into these writings. I am realizing it may be appearing that is the case to outsiders. That was never the intent!

APPRECIATION and ACCEPTANCE...Appreciation for the knowledge that I have always made an attempt to do my very, very best my entire life. I have done everything that I could do, in good faith and with my maximum effort to process and act on the information and facts as I saw them at that place in time. I have performed in the arena and I have dared to take risks. I have worked very hard. I have trusted. I have always strived to be fair. I have been responsible. I have been generous in ways that I could. I have not hesitated to pull the trigger, many times. And, this place, this location, this circumstance, this situation, this is where I am. There must be a reason I have been guided here. God has led me here for reasons I cannot possibly realize or know. It is totally up to me to play this out.

This is MY journey. I shall never damn, blame, regret, question, or curse where I am in this moment. Rather, I choose to celebrate my circumstance and trust, as always, in what God plans for me. HE has all the wisdom, answers, and power. I accept, with gratitude and humility, the path I am seemingly destined to be on. Only God sees all. And I, as I perceive myself to be an evolving and committed and trusting follower, shall endeavor to make the most of my "current" situation and grow, yet again, to become all that I can be in this incarnation.

For whatever reasons, I am being called upon to do more. I choose to again, be proactive. Challenge is to not be feared, but rather embraced and acted upon with conviction and commitment. I pray for the strength, determination and courage to allow this newest obstacle and evolution to go forward. I am not, and never have been, a "victim". I will continue to choose and strive to live my life as a person who is stimulated, challenged, active, involved, committed and growth-oriented. I accept God's will be done. Amen.

In many ways, I know I am truly blessed in that I have always, my entire life, been able to go so much deeper than many of my contemporaries. It seems I have an awareness that speaks to me. I feel so fortunate in that I never, ever have given up. I just step back, patiently observe, analyze, listen, and process. Then I act. I have always had a vision and trust in "my plan", as God sees it, on this earth. It seems to me that so many people just spend their entire lives reacting to what life seems to toss their way. They just appear unaware or content to drift aimlessly in the wind and let happenstance dictate where they end up. They set no goals, they put out minimum effort, they choose the easy way. They avoid testing themselves. They just exist, like an insect or a worm.

They examine nothing. They risk little. They refuse to accept responsibility. They want "security". They prefer to be blameless in everything. They just tread water their entire lives and then bask in their good fortune when they know, at some level of consciousness, that they are impostors. What they "achieved" was all just blind luck. They actually believe it was all about them. What hubris. They live shallow, simple, unexamined, empty lives.

They did not have the fortitude to push themselves with a maximum effort, not even once! They never knew what they were made of and at the end they ask, in their bewilderment, what was the point? What did life mean? And tragically, they never had even a clue! So for them, there really never was a point! The golden gift of life, that glorious opportunity, was wasted or at least, truly unrealized and diminished.

To me, that is not being truly alive. That demonstrates no gratitude. But, I grant them their journey. Choices. Yet, I really feel blessed that I believe myself to be on a different and deeper level. I do feel more evolved and I say that not with arrogance, but rather deep appreciation. I truly want to grow and to continue to do so my entire life. I really am trying, every single day. So, I feel different and more fortunate and more developed in a spiritual way than most people in my circle.

Perhaps all people feel this way, I cannot know. I speak only for myself. I just have my observations. I also have my own private relationship with God and I realize many other people have theirs also, and that is as it should be. We are all children of God and special and unique in our own way in His eyes. How blessed and humbled and appreciative and thankful and accepting we should all strive to be.

ESSAY 51:
A Concept of Time, a Fishing Analogy

What is time? When one is going fishing in the present moment, he is also remembering those times in the past when he caught a fish. He is also looking into the future at that exact same "time", for he is anticipating catching a large fish that he does not even yet know exists. Yet in an instant that "future" and "past" also becomes the PRESENT. So there is no longer a distinction. That fish that existed in the PAST, for it was known to exist, came into the present when you first saw it and melded with the future at that moment when you presently just hooked it. So actually the past, present and future all existed for you at precisely that same moment! All that changed was your perspective of time. So really, what is time?

ESSAY 52:
Validation of all these essays?

I have written many essays to date. I have composed these from percolations arising deep within. I have sent many to my children and a few to other persons I perceived would give some feedback. I have received next to none. That has been very instructive to me. It proves to me that I am on a different level from anyone I know. However, I have been doing some reading. I have visited some writings from Viktor Frankl and Tolstoy. I wrote my essays before I had read or studied these authors, thus they are pure in original thought from me. These were both of the school of existentialism or logo-therapy.

The point is, they and I are on the exact same page as to what I believe to be true! I understand everything they are saying and I have even taken it deeper, for me. These are great thinkers and I have similar ideas as did they. I am at the soul level, for me. We are on the same vibrational frequency and that is all I have been seeking, to be aware that there have been and most assuredly must be others who get what I am saying. It tells me I am onto something significant and I feel it. I know I must try to share these writings while I have some remaining time to do so. With their writings, I know I can go deeper because I want and desire to do so.

Now I am aware that to send these essays to anyone I know is not feasible or productive. It is like I am speaking to them in some ancient language or foreign tongue and they are too uncomfortable to even admit they have no clue what I am talking about. Or, they disagree with me completely. That is OK, of course. So, I will write for myself and perhaps publish at some future date. I do know that to write all these profound (to me) writings and not share them is beyond reason. Why not plant seeds for other seekers to expand upon? Thus, more awareness is raised and my life has more meaning even after I am gone. I can go with a satisfied smile and be content knowing I put in a solid effort to try to speak from beyond the grave. Thus, if I accomplish this, I am ready to have my rest.

ESSAY 53:
Faith and Consciousness

I have a dear friend who passed away suddenly after a three month illness from a brain tumor. He was an atheist at worst and an agnostic at best. He believed that man does have a "consciousness" but there is no "supreme entity" per se. I would propose that it is not possible for a consciousness to arise spontaneously from an unconscious origin. There must be a Supreme all encompassing Consciousness from which all states of such can arise. A chicken cannot just arise spontaneously from a dormant lifeless rock.

As I look into the eyes of a dog or any animal, how can I not be aware that a consciousness exists in that living, breathing animal? As I watch our birds go about their daily exercises of just living and trying to stay alive, how can they not have an awareness, albeit a more primitive one? They must pay attention to their every action just to stay alive. They can sense danger, food sources, a mate, protecting their young, etc. How is that not a certain state of consciousness beyond simple primitive instinct? I told my dying friend that it is my belief that we are presented with obstacles and dire circumstances to test our faith. I got no feedback on this from him which leads me to believe he did not agree per se. Or, he just never really thought about it. His only response was that "I have a great mind and should continue to write".

I believe God just kept trying to get my friend's attention. He and his wife were subjected to so many accumulating and increasingly gut-wrenching experiences with their two sons. It just kept getting worse and worse. There were three surreal events as he got to the end that gave him every opportunity to change his thinking about God. His oldest son carelessly took his own life. His other son came within minutes of killing him, his own father! Finally, God gave my friend one last chance to "get it". God knows how good a person this man was. He was a remarkable, loving and talented human being. I just pray that he finally understood the big picture at the end.

I just believe we all have our opportunities in life to "figure it out". Of course, we each must do this for ourselves. Or not. Each person's answer must be his own. The common reality, I do believe, is that God is ONE and every living organism or bit of matter, is but a miniscule portion of that ONE. I liken it to a burning candle. As we live our life our candle burns brightly. As we enter our winter, the breezes become colder and the flame begins to flicker. It starts to weaken and grow dimmer. Soon enough, the candle burns out. The smoke rises from the end of the wick and winds its way outward and upward. The flame ceases to exist but that energy alters in form. It fades into and becomes part of the atmosphere. It becomes ONE with it.

So it is with the human soul. It departs the assigned body and becomes ONE as it is integrated into the vapors of the ethereal mist of eternity. If we are not able to grasp this concept deep in our souls, we are, to my thinking, no more than a lifeless, very temporary mass of protoplasm. Our lives were of no lasting meaning. We were nothing, actually.

If this dear friend did not come to believe this, even at his end, then for all he achieved in his life, he still lacked a most significant understanding and point of life itself, in my opinion. So, I would think that he must go through even more at some future place and time to find his true salvation. My belief is my belief and I state these things believing this at my core. Everything that happens to us has a purpose and a meaning and we MUST pay attention!!! We either get it or we do not. If we do not, more work must be done. But no matter what work is required, it is never-ending. That is the entire point. We must continually be tested to keep growing, evolving, believing, becoming, approaching but never obtaining enlightenment or attainment. God is total and absolute enlightenment and to not believe in HIM is to never get higher than your current station. You are arrested and dormant and truly done. I do not ever want to be done!

Yes, when it is time, I will take my rest. But I do so looking forward to my next assignment. I do feel I have kept my integrity and done myself proud during my brief visit on my stopover this time. I have lived with a strong work ethic, honesty, conviction, passion, deep belief, gratitude, service, empathy and enough humility. I have faced every test as best I could with the skills and tools I had at my disposal at the time. I have paid attention and processed events in my life as deeply as I could humanly do. I have sought out and found my own answers to my own questions for me. What else can a person ask to achieve in one lifetime? I feel I have done my work and shall continue to do so. Perhaps build some equity as long as I am granted the opportunity by my Divine Maker. I feel truly blessed. I have enough. Truly.

ESSAY 54:
Our True Essence

Following is a synopsis of portions of previous essays I have composed. It is 2:40 am. on Sat. in February in Key Largo. This kinda sums it up for me. Man needs to "graduate" or evolve his thinking. 99% of people live their entire lives in the physical sense. They are into their egos in that they believe their physical being is really all they have, all they are. They fail to go deep within to realize or become aware that the physical is so very temporary. The only thing that is lasting is the spirit. It is energy and energy cannot ever be destroyed.

By coming to the realization that our lives are just temporarily leased to us, we do not own them, for they disappear and our essence, our real permanence exists only in our spirits, our souls. At our arrival, we are assigned a name and we assume an identity. When you start to really learn to acknowledge this fact, you gradually release yourself from ego-centric desires. You begin to really see for the first time. You are not as attached to possessions, nor do you need them for "security" per se. You do not desire all the trappings of a fake and materialistic life. Less becomes more and less is enough. You recognize the connections with all living things and see that they are just briefly visiting too. You become more empathic and understanding of the travails of others. You want to be of service and live a life of meaning and live it with love. You come to learn that it is not a competition for we are all in this together.

You do not judge. You do not need to "win" in that your gain is at the expense of another's losing. The thing is, once you truly know and feel and accept the temporary nature of everything around you, you surrender and you gain faith. You know we are all connected and ONE with all that was, is, and will be, forever into eternity. You become more appreciative and serene in your daily activities. You know that to "die' is to merely move on to your next assignment, directed by the Divine. Everything starts to make more sense in that you see the perfection in the entire system.

I was blessed to observe the physical death of the three year old daughter of very dear friends. Her organs were shutting down due to spina bifida. I was 31 years old. I was with her on a hospital gurney with a nurse. Her parents knew she was dying and did not want to be there at that moment. I did. She was dressed only in panties. Her body was totally bare of clothes or a sheet. I was looking down at her and suddenly I witnessed and felt this energy. Her left big toe was slightly beyond her other foot in length. Instantly I saw and heard this "whoosh". A white vapor shot up from the tip of her left big toe and enveloped her entire body in a mini-flash. It shot up from the top of her head and exited at the apex of the room, where the walls and ceiling met at the closest corner. It was clearly pure energy.

It was her young, innocent and pure unspoiled soul, her spirit leaving a body that was defective and she was now free. I instantly observed salt crystals form a crust in the canthus and corners of both eyes. What was two moist eyes before was now salt. And I experienced pure and Divine peace in that very moment. I had just been chosen to witness her ascension and I was spellbound by the beauty and wonder of it all! It was so obvious that her spirit had departed and there was just a shell left behind.

That defective and seriously flawed body was of no use anymore to her for she was released from it. It was such a beautiful and reassuring event to witness. If I had blinked I would have missed it. I asked the attending nurse if she saw anything and she said she had not. She missed it. I was blessed. I felt the correctness and order and beauty of her passage. This precious young being was liberated! It was the most awesome experience! Beyond profound!

To live in your spiritual essence is to live in a bit of heaven while on earth. Obviously, heaven is a state of lasting Nirvana whereas here is merely our proving ground, our test. Here we strive to arrive at that state where things just do not affect you in the same way as when you break away from the temporary physical and live in the enlightenment of the spiritual realm. Other people can sense your centeredness and calmness and serenity within yourself. Our hectic society does not allow the environment to easily get to this.

It takes time and acute observation and deep introspection to reach this awareness. Of course we can never completely arrive to this place. But the seeking is part of our earthly journey and that striving is its own reward. Once you truly accept that you shall discard your physical body soon enough, you will be OK and accepting of what mysteries and new adventures lie ahead.

The more actualized you become the higher your energy vibrations become. Thus, when you proceed onward to the next level, your higher frequency propels you to a more advanced incarnation in some form in some place. There, you do more work and thus move forward through eternity. The spirit is where all things that matter and last truly reside. So, our challenge becomes to get to know and feel this truism in this brief and temporary physical presence and go within and live in the spirit world more permanently as you are also of this physical world.

If you suffer great losses but you have discovered how to reside in your spirit world, you will have everything you shall ever need. All will always be OK. The journey is the reward.

If you want "proof" of the concept of living in the spirit realm vs. the physical one, simply observe by looking deeply into the eyes of a young dog, just beyond the puppy stage. What do you see? What do you feel? You see pure love, pure trust, pure joy at being alive and being in your loving presence! By such a simple observation you get all the answers you need. The most profound answers to everything are right in front of you, IF you just pay Attention! DOG>GOD>DOG. Animals tell us so much. Their spirits are so pure and unfiltered. You can see and feel a dog's love for you at the soul level. You are acutely aware of this connection. So it is with God's love for you, not for your body but for your soul. Hopefully, this love is reciprocated by you to Him. Many bodies are not so attractive yet the soul and spirit of that person can be most beautiful.

When a dog is dying, they know it instinctively. They sense it and do not show fear in their eyes. They look up at their master with calmness, acceptance, wisdom, serenity, appreciation, and pure love and trust. They show sadness and pure love at the same time. And they are ready to go. They do not fight it. They will sigh and can almost smile at you at the very moment of physical death. They are telling us that everything is OK, and they are thanking you.

It is really a most beautiful and natural thing to witness and feel, although the pain of those left behind is beyond words at the time. Then when we have sufficiently grieved their physical loss, we eventually are left with the best memories of such pure love and joy by having them in our lives and we experience great gratitude for having shared our lives with them. We also know that God is love and love is forever, so we shall most assuredly be together again.

So again, learn to devote your energies to developing and experiencing life's experiences at the spirit level. The rewards are permanent and everlasting throughout all eternity. Everything will start to make perfect sense to you and you will just know that all is as it is meant to be, and it is OK. ...Be at Peace...

ESSAY 55:
Authenticity as Essential for Spiritual Growth

I believe that by recognizing, acknowledging, accepting, and then honoring and ultimately celebrating the TRUE feelings God gives uniquely to each one of us is a very necessary growth and maturation process in order to develop a much deeper spiritual awareness in one's life. I also believe this is but one way of many but it is the singular fundamental process to potentiate many other venues that lead's one deeper in this quest and yearning to go as deep as one can possibly go in a singular lifetime.

If one cannot lead an authentic life with oneself first, then the mask must be worn an entire lifetime. How emptying and wasteful and sad is that?! A missed opportunity that I believe is the Divine essence of being blessed to be born as a human being. This blessing is meant to be honored, nurtured, developed and celebrated. Given individual choice, this becomes our test.

A spiritual avenue to me, is to be able to give and receive true love of another human being, ideally, and also to be able to give and receive love of animals. Love, in any form, is essential. Love of nature, all God's creatures, all that HE/SHE has created. See the mastery and beauty in everything!

Appreciation, charity, helpfulness, stewardship, compassion, struggle, suffering, loss, hardship, music, nature, forgiveness, non-judgemental, acceptance, surrender, understanding the big picture, loving life. These all contribute to spiritual growth. It is like we are presented with all these daily tests and the more comfortable and accepting we become with these, the more centered we are and thus more spiritual and evolved we become. No need to be afraid when one is spiritually centered. One can be concerned of course, but that concern ideally leads one to take some sort of proactive measures. A serene calmness comes to exist within and shows in all that you do and all whom you are.

Very importantly, a person cannot be a truly spiritual being without having a moral compass and a conscience. One that is congruent with God's teachings and His lessons. This is axiomatic and I believe this with all my heart and soul. Being spiritual is like living a mortal life with one's soul comfortably on his sleeve.

I also believe others on a similar wavelength tend to gravitate to one another. They just seem to find each other. To me, a true gift of a life being lived well is being blessed to recognize and be appreciative of people such as that in our midst. These types of individuals enrich the human experience. I try to learn something from every person I meet. Every encounter teaches me something. These people grow me and I like to believe I grow them. I love the stimulation of attempting to be truly aware in every situation and environment I find myself in. I so much relish my technicolor moments and truly feel blessed when they occur for me.

ESSAY 56:

Perfection, and it's price... Parenting

Perfection, or the constant seeking of it, has its price. It can exert a very severe toll. There exists a trap of life there. If you are a perfectionist, you cannot, by definition, allow yourself to fail-ever! And when you do fail, and you will because we all fail at certain times in our lives, you can tend to lose confidence in yourself. Rather, it is much more healthy to re-frame "failure" as a minor and necessary temporary set-back. Thus, you can gain confidence, not lose it, as you navigate through the hurdles life places in front of all of us. To become successful at something or in life, it is required that you fail at times along the way. Failure is a much better teacher than success ever was.

A huge problem with a perfectionist is they set an impossible standard for themselves. If their parents demand and expect perfection and nothing the child does is ever good enough, the stage is set for bad outcomes for all. The child wants to be loved. The child wants to please and not disappoint the source of that love and security, ie. their parents. If the child is taught that it is not acceptable to make mistakes, several things can result. The child will not dare try anything new or challenging for fear of not doing it correctly. They will just "lose it" when a mistake is made. They will spend way too much time and effort on mastering a task at the expense of losing necessary balance in their life. They can become driven and obsessive.

Oftentimes, they can eventually deduce that they cannot possibly please their parents so why even bother or try? They can separate from them emotionally and then physically. They can become weary of the demands placed on them, especially when their friends do not seem to have these. They can become rebellious. They can challenge. If they perceive themselves as having no control in their lives to experiment, test or make their own decisions, you can lose them. They will begin to make their own decisions. Unfortunately, these are usually poor ones just to show their parents that you (parents) cannot control EVERYTHING in their young lives!

They can get into the wrong crowd at school, children who are also rebelling. They can become anorexic. That way, it is they who claim some control vs. that of their patents. They can get into alcohol and drugs, to escape the pressures or to "shove it" to their parents. They were never permitted to be "bad" sometimes, by their parents, so to prove they are not always as good as their parents believe, they go to the other extreme. A girl may become pregnant or be promiscuous. Or run away. Boys get into fights, become poor students, smoke, drink, drug, get inked up, run with the wrong crowd. Oftentimes, parents who had little control over their own upbringing tend to pass their unexamined baggage onto their children. The parents did not do their work thus cede their unfinished business to the next generation.

People who do not take any risks know they have never allowed themselves to be tested. They were too afraid. They sought the easy and safe way each time they were challenged. They backed down. Thus, if by some good fortune or luck they do achieve success, they know deep down at some level that they are imposters. They can have some deep insecurities knowing the truth of their "success". They can overreach and bully and try to mask these deep feelings of insecurity. They can overestimate and over-rate their skills and abilities. They fear exposure.

ESSAY 57:

What is Truth, and why the younger generation may not want to hear it, from you

The younger generation simply does not want to hear it. My generation is old. We are on the way out. Make way for the new. Things are different now. They are going to fix it. They are going to do it better. How can they possibly place any credence in what we have to say? What do we know? We fail to care about all the modern gadgets that they have at their disposal to keep them on top of all things. They fail to realize that these instruments and this technology does zero to solve the problems or answer the questions of life.

Thus, since we do not get all caught up and blindly embrace and submerse ourselves in all this latest technology, we are perceived as less than. Being less than, what we have to say is of little importance. Of course, we were raised in a different era. Our reality is so different from their reality. How could they possibly relate to what we have to say? They cannot. Only when they have repeated the mistakes and suffered enough and seen enough and lived long enough could they possibly have any desire to examine the words of wisdom of those generations who have preceded them. All generations must learn the same basic lessons of life. And on and on and on....

So, for a 75 year old man to try to be relative to their children in certain ways in their 30's and 40's is just not possible. How can a younger person possibly understand the messages from their elderly father when they have had totally different experiences and are a generation younger? These words will have no meaning until/unless these children truly grow up and become fully functioning mature adults with enough spiritual awareness to even seek or know there are answers out there for them. I have hope but no actual expectations from any of them at this latter stage of my life.

I have lived my life. I release them to give it their best shot. I can see where they are doing things differently than I would be. Some seem destined to make some mistakes I can foresee each of them making. That is OK. It is their turn to conquer the world. There is nothing I can say to them at this stage of their lives that would change one single thing. And I have no right to voice my opinion. They may be correct, they may not be. Thus, my continual learning. Detach, detach, detach, albeit with hope and love.

As stated before in previous essays, one cannot offer "advice" to your "children", even at their being in middle age themselves, unless they request it. And they do not often request it. To offer it would only be resented, and discounted very highly! So I refrain and restrain myself. Thus, I resolve I shall never, ever offer it, unsolicited. And I am of the opinion it will almost never be solicited. They are on their own paths, as are we all. Who am I to interfere with their choices and their consequences to the decisions they have made and are making? They are on their own, as are all of God's creation. Some few figure it out but most never do.

And for those very few that do arrive at their correct answers, they must do the work, as I have done and am trying to continue to do. There is a price to be paid in doing this work. Nothing of true and lasting value comes cheap. Pain must be endured, losses, suffering, doubts, failure, uncertainty...all are necessary. So, I have finally arrived at a place of total peace with my children. I have released myself from any expected outcomes. They are who they are. I am who I am. I am at peace with myself at age 75 (and way before that). I love my children so I cheer them on as best I can.

Only when they are much older can they possibly have a clue as to what I am talking about. And those who have not done the work will never understand one iota of what I am referring to in this or any of the many essays and axioms I have taken the time to write. They were intended originally for my children but I have come to the realization they are better shared with those who are wise enough and curious enough to want to have some miniscule potential guidance along their journey of life.

I am not so arrogant or insecure as to need validation or approval, in that what I have to say matters to any true seeker out there. I do believe that my words will resonate with some, and hopefully many, but that is out of my control. All I can do is make an honest effort. I can live with the results. And, that is more than OK with me. Again, arrive at your own truths, as I have done with mine. That is my challenge to my children. Grow up. Be an adult. Pull the trigger. Be responsible. But care enough about your God given gift of life to ask the relevant questions! Can or will they ever do it? I can always hope. I will be long gone, not my issue any more. Actually, never my issue once I addressed it for myself. It is now theirs, or not. The ball is now in their court. Ah, that marvelous game of life!! Gotta love it!! Thank you God!!!

ESSAY 58:
Faith

It is my belief that the reason a person suffers from an impossible situation such as a terminal illness or a great loss is to test one's faith. The more severe the circumstance, the more profound the test becomes. And profound tests, if addressed directly and absorbed in the correct way, can result in great spiritual growth. It becomes extremely difficult to grow to the point of surrender, acceptance, belief, and faith in a higher power that in the end, there is no "end." This current torment will hopefully, eventually become reframed in that one will understand that it is all OK. OK in the sense that this pain and suffering, if met head on in the correct manner can lead and will lead to great rewards. These rewards will come to be realized in this lifetime and ultimately be carried beyond this incarnation.

One will come to realize that every single entity, happenstance, event, circumstance, etc. is all temporary. Life itself is very temporary. Every single thing is temporary on this physical planet. One will become aware that the one single thing that is not temporary is the spirit, for it transcends all physical existence. And a developed and acute sense of spirit, or soul comes from faith developed and arising from within, that by necessity, must be tested for true growth to occur. A person who is not tested cannot possibly grow spiritually. And to grow spiritually has to be the only way to evolve at the soul level to a higher plane.

Thus, when one suffers, as much as we do not seek it, the test is undertaken. How will I respond? How will I reframe this calamity so as to reach the point where I accept this fate and do not question it any longer. No more why me, what if, I wish I had done this or that, etc. One must eventually reach the conclusion that this is where I am and I shall grow from this challenge. I do not understand it, I do not like it, I do not want it, but I will do my very best to deal with it till I am no longer able. Along the way, I will become more empowered as I learn more about my spiritual progression by the way I navigate this severe situation. And if an earlier physical death is the end result of this test, so be it.

In fighting this battle, I am becoming much stronger spiritually even as I have become more weak physically. And I am well aware that to be spiritually strong is far more important and lasting than being physically strong. I refuse to become a victim for I am in complete control of the manner in which I chose to learn and grow from this. Each day is an opportunity to show myself that I am becoming stronger than this disease. This disease has given me the opportunity to grow spiritually much stronger than perhaps I would have, had this not happened to me. For whatever reason, this is my very own personal individual burden that was "assigned" to me in this incarnation on this planet called Earth. It is temporary. I have no fear, for I shall move to a higher vibrational level as a result of this and that is something I am very comfortable with, for I have faith. This happenstance did not weaken me, it strengthened me.

ESSAY 59:
My Beginnings, money and fate

Being from a rather backward and proud southern state, (it is much better now) I am so like the many people who grew up there many, many decades ago. We do not feel we are worthy or deserving of good fortune. And, if we do have opportunities to achieve this, we tend to let up on the throttle and end up with less. I did so much better than my father and ALL my relatives. So, whom am I to expect to deserve more? So, I did end up with less materialistically than I was capable of.

I was listening to a friend of my wife's tonight and it was so emblematic of life. She will be well off financially from her forthcoming divorce and she has since hooked up with another man who is also of very substantial means. She is so very set. Her ex came from wealth and he is also very financially secure and yet he is a royal A-hole. I have been a very hard worker all my life and I am a decent enough guy and yet, here I am, with much less than others who have worked and dreamed so much lower than I. Life can sometimes appear to be a real crock. Pure randomness and happenstance. There can sometimes tend to be little rhyme nor reason to any of it, in many instances. However, that is a surface observation. It is much more complicated than that.

But, I do not curse my life at all. It is what it is. I accept my life and do not lament any of it. I feel truly blessed for I have been severely tested multiple times and I never have complained or resented my situations. These circumstances navigated thru have strengthened and made me who I am. I feel proud of the strength of my character and the convictions I have. I do know many things (really nothing) and I do have peace of mind. What do I have to complain about, really?! I accept who I am and where I am. I have a friend with a multi-million dollar portfolio, yet he complains and moans about a few measly dollars. He frequently loses sleep over it and oftentimes cannot eat. The money and fear of losing it controls his life. He does not learn to just let it go and get on with it, ie. his life. He has no peace. I do have peace so I ask, who is richer? I thank you God. Amen

ESSAY 60:
Nature of Man

This is such a complicated subject to dwell upon. It is a continuation, of sorts, of previous essays. I am just attempting to make some deeper sense of mankind and the state of affairs that exist today. In doing so, I am just trying to figure it out and reach some personal conclusions. A question I ponder: Will war always exist and will it have a happy ending? The answer is yes, it will always exist and no, it will not have a happy ending...IF we continue as we are! I do not believe that human beings seek war by their nature.

I do believe there are insecure people who have agendas for themselves that place them in positions of great power and influence. These individuals will do anything and use any means to get what they want. They lead powerful international corporations that destroy people's lives and rape the environment. They lead governments that stop at nothing to gain power and influence. They dupe their citizens and penalize or eliminate those who question their actions or authority.

I observe that certain countries NEVER initiate a war. They will fight when they are forced to do so, when they are threatened in some way. Thus, the desire for war is NOT innate in humans. However, in our present times, more and more people are being threatened by so many things out of their control. Natives cannot earn a decent living so immigrants are a threat to them. There is not enough housing for everyone. Food and water are becoming more scarce. These people are not one of us, they are different, they are thus a direct threat and they are not welcome. I will fight them if needed to rid them from being a threat.

The immigrants. They just want what everyone wants. Live in peace. Provide for their families. Work and play and practice their faith. They have been displaced by war or climate events. They have already lost everything that mattered to them, so what more can they lose other than their life? So what, my life has no value any longer anyway. I will fight you to get my share, which I am entitled to as a human being, just like you. Thus, more conflicts, leading to more wars.

This planet is now entering the scarcity period. Weather catastrophes, fuel, water and food shortages, CO_2 atmospheric build-up, overcrowding, less usable land, not enough housing, etc. Thus, there is not enough for everybody to get their needs met. So continuing conflicts are inevitable...till the end.

Can we, as the human race, avoid this fate? In my opinion, the absolute only way to prevent our own demise is to understand completely how non-sustainable our course has become. Power, greed, domination, destruction, these things must stop! And very sadly and with resignation I can state that human beings must and will suffer greatly in these present and coming times. They must now pay the supreme price of all the suffering that must occur to change the direction of the human species. We need great calamities to wake us up and these have an excellent chance to accelerate in these "modern" times. With a failure of leadership in our present divisive society and government, I see chaos, extreme divisions, power struggles, use of fear and intimidation, anger, fights for survival all around the world, with the USA right in the middle of all this, of course. Gotta protect our national interests (special interests)!

Tragically, the world is ripe for turmoil and upheaval and it is now time for this to happen. It is similar to a catastrophic fire in the forest. It will destroy most everything on the surface, but deeper, out of the ashes arise new life and new beginnings. This earth, the peoples, these values, these divisions must change and the only way this can happen is to completely destroy the ways of the past. That means complete and total chaos must occur and much destruction of property and life and existing systems must happen. When it is finally over, when enough suffering has occurred, when very little remains, (Aleppo), if it is meant to be, the survivors will come together and cooperate in order to survive together. If they fail to do so, they will fall aside and the earth will rebalance itself with man having eliminated themselves from the equation.

I am not a pessimist by nature, but this is where I see mankind at this point in time. Actually, when I remove myself from the surface and look down from way above, this just seems so very obvious. Everything is becoming aligned for this to happen sooner rather than later. The patterns are very clear. For me, I have complete trust that what is destined to happen will happen as it is supposed to. I have zero problem with whatever the "solution "becomes. I do know change can be difficult but becomes easier when you reach the point of total and complete trust in the process. God's will be done.

BTW, people should just keep living their lives, for the future has always been an unknown and an uncertainty. Do not bail on life because of what "may" happen. Just stay vigilant, protect your loved ones as much as possible, get your learnings and pass it on. Try to continue to retain some hope.

ESSAY 61:
Moral responsibility for one's actions

If a person is unaware of his actions causing unnecessary harm to others, is he an evil person? Is he responsible for his actions? I would say he is responsible but not evil. What about on a spiritual level? Should a person be held accountable for his ignorance? He has to be in a just world, because his stupidity has caused great harm to many fellow human beings. Life is not fair, nor could we expect it to be. That is part of our test. How do we handle all that being a living human being entails?

ESSAY 62:
Obliviousness

Many are so oblivious to truths that are very evident to me, that they are totally oblivious to the fact they are oblivious!! So many people just live their lives so unaware and semi-conscious, or unconscious even. Of course, I too am not aware of many things, but I feel very aware of matters I should be conscious of. I feel confident I function at a level higher than many others.

Thus, I believe for me, I am on a correct path for my life. I am observant and thoughtful in my observations and decisions for my life and the way I live it. I am true to myself and to my deep convictions about the correct way to live for me. I observe others and sometimes am just amazed at their manner of living and choices they are making. I feel very fortunate that I just see things differently. I am saddened but also detached directly from their choices. I just feel these people are somewhat primitive in many ways and realize there are so many levels of development in the human race.

I do believe myself to be further along than many I have encountered in my life thus far. But I am aware that I know very little. Yet, I am comfortable with my progression. I am a work in progress, as are we all. Or some of us. Again, obliviousness is very prevalent. Many are searching but I feel I am validating much more than I am searching. I feel very comfortable in my own temporary earth skin. I try to not allow the actions or inactions of others get to me so much. Thus, I try not to judge or be attached to outcomes for I recognize we all have our own perceptions and realities.

I just am very comfortable in what I conclude in my examinations and observations of life. It works for me and for that, I feel very blessed. I know I am doing the work on a daily basis to ease my mind and question everything and the answers I discover make sense to me. At least, I care enough to continually ask my questions, seek my answers, and form my spiritual conclusions. Spiritual is the only answer that ever makes any sense to me on this beautiful planet we have absurdly and selfishly been ruining since mankind has arrived.

My hope is that many more people can find a better way for them in this world and gain some insights from some of the words I have written.

ESSAY 63:
Spiritual Connections... Subjective or Objective?

I am pondering if a spiritual connection is subjective or objective. I feel there may be degrees of spirituality that fall short of true soul level spirituality. As an example, in my and a female friend's case from many years ago, we were of similar views about many things, but I feel my spiritual awareness was on a different frequency than hers. Not better, just my own vs. her own, as it must be, I do surmise. She chose to terminate a pregnancy, abort a healthy, precious gift of her Creator because it was" not convenient" for her to birth her very own child at that time. That is the antithesis of a spiritual being, in my awareness of what spirituality is all about. Also, she had denied two very precious things from her husband as a price to pay for being her "husband". Both these things had always been, for him, a direct source of emotional and spiritual nourishment.

After some deep private discussions with her husband, I concluded he was the bigger person because he loved her and he had been willing to compensate and had eventually reframed these facts to better use these denials from her to be a deeper spiritual test for him to overcome. In my opinion, much of what his wife did had narcissistic and selfish origins, rather than spiritual one's. To have a child out of wedlock would have spoiled her image as the perfect, desirable woman who does no wrong. The woman who was mortified her DUI's would be discovered, even when close female friend's confided to her their missteps, she never admitted she was guilty of the very same things.

She was not demonstrably emotional in that she seldom teared up very easily, even rarely, compared to many women, and even some men, that I have known. She could have difficulty dealing with others' perceived transgressions. She would sometimes struggle growing beyond them. Yet, she was kind to animals and to many people. She was a giving person and had a warm and loving heart to her husband, children, family and friends. She was a doer of good deeds for others. She could be counted on.

To me, her spiritual quest seemed to say she was trying but she had much work to do and I do not believe she could possibly attain the level she claimed to seek in her current lifetime. Yes, on some things, but no on other things. This sounds judgmental, and it probably is, but that is not the intent. It is meant as an observation that seems to validate to me that we all have our own paths and choices and as an observer of others, I learn and draw my conclusions from these behaviors I am privy to. The path she chooses is not the path I choose. There is no right or wrong. There are differences and these are to be respected and not judged. What do I know? What do any of us really know?

So I conclude that spiritual awareness and development to be with, and of, the ONE is a very individual thing. Some grow towards it, some have no clue what I am even talking about. Each of us who are attempting awareness gets closer by different ways and means. Oftentimes, it takes a singular life-altering experience to jump-start us. Sometimes, it is something that was just there from our earliest awareness, as has been my case. My message of early awareness is I have always been a seeker and observer and active participant in my own life, rather than just "wait for something to happen".

Each meaningful event is something I think deeply about. I ponder it, I reflect on it, I reach conclusions about it. Some would say it is too much. Pretty far out. It certainly may be true. For me it is not. For them, whatever. No matter. When I am ready, I come to accept the current challenge and even eventually look forward to what action I shall take to maximize my learning from it. All this deepens and further reinforces, rather than weakens, my spiritual connection to the ONE.

A Question....? Many hunters love nature and have kind hearts, yet "harvest" animals. Physicians who save lives seek out and enjoy killing animals. I understand the need to thin the herds, etc. I just do not get the spirituality in killing.

Life is just so many things, in so many different ways, in so many different circumstances, to so many people, to all of us. What a dance it is and how do we discover the right beat that we can dance to? What is the rhythm? God is a real "stinker". How cunning He is! What a game He plays with us! May as well enjoy it for what it is.

ESSAY 64:
We are Here To Help

I am of the belief we are here to do everything we can to use our gifts and talents to help others. For me, this is a primary reason for living! I do know, because so many patients have told me so, that they have had the best dental experience of their life with my treating them. Please do not leave! I am told this much too often to be discounted or minimized by me. It is very evident that God has sent me a message loud and clear, that dentistry is where I am to serve my fellow human beings. We are all in this game of life together and the more aware and evolved ones know that we must help each other in any way we can.

I am so very fortunate because I have always known certain things that many others do not appear to know. They have not learned that to recognize and devote much of your attention, talents, and energy and try to serve others and thus to serve HIM is a primary mission and purpose in life. I am so thankful to God that I have seen and continue to see this so vividly! There is absolutely zero doubt about how I intend to devote the rest of my life to God through the ministry of my performing dentistry for the remainder of my capable working life!!

For me to go backward into myself, ego, material comfort, and "relaxing" is the antithesis of who I am and who I have always been! I just refuse to squander and surrender my life-long well earned learning curve so I can just place myself on the shelf. I will NEVER discard my mission in life! NEVER! Most people have no clue what true passion and a life mission even means. God led me to this place in my life. I am 1000% convinced of this! So many events, over 65 years in the making, had to occur for me to be here, in this position, in this locale, at this moment in time. I ask myself, has my life been a help to others and have I had a meaningful and positive impact on my interactions with whom I have come in contact with? I can answer absolutely, YES! At least, I have put forth a sincere effort.

I must continue to educate myself and be qualified to do what I do. I have gifts. I have talents. I have knowledge. I have experience. I have communication skills. I have maturity, empathy, and wisdom. I simply must do all that is necessary for me to re-enter my profession. I have been retired for several years now. I am rested and yet I am restless. I must get back in the game while I still have the energy and desire to do so. God will guide me in the correct direction. If it is meant to be, it shall be. When I am meant to be done, He will tell me. Meanwhile, off I go, yet again. I am entering my last lap and I intend to sprint to the end. We shall see how my final race ends.

ESSAY 65:
"Ethics"

It has been stated that " Ethics are relative". Initially, I vehemently rejected that premise. But now I am wondering. In my profession. I will not violate a tooth surface if it appears sound and no caries is evident. However, another operator will see a deep groove that "may" become a future cavity and choose to fill it to possibly prevent "potential" future caries, to his mind. Who is correct? Either, or both? I know what is correct and ethical for me.

A hunter justifies killing animals to prevent potential disease and overgrazing and thus starvation of masses of animals. Thus, by killing some, he is saving many. They supposedly do not suffer a long prolonged death due to starvation. That is ethical to him. To me, to kill a healthy animal for "sport" is not ethical. So, are ethics relative? I do believe something is morally right or it is not. Everything else is but an excuse to justify wrong behaviors. This is a fuzzy question for sure. I do not know the answer to this. The only conclusion I can reach is that one must be true to his personal values and beliefs. Only God can judge reasons for behaviors. It is not my call.

ESSAY 66:
MY SOUL

I am in intimate touch with my divinity. My spirit is something I am comfortable being fused with in an active way. I can sense very strongly when I am in the presence of another person similar to myself. Our energy frequencies are in tune. We each must strive to get to this place in our own way, but to continue our existential development, we must always be seeking, till the end. I have total serenity within me. Of course, I do get upset and frustrated at times. However, I can always go within and find my peace in this chaotic world. I am very safe there for I feel totally connected to my ONE-ness!

I sleep soundly. Always have been so fortunate. Never have I taken any sleep aids in my life! My wife and I are extremely blessed in that we have many, many friends, all over the world. One main reason I do believe is that we are very comfortable within ourselves. We project that comfort and confidence with our interactions with others. People really do enjoy our company. And we certainly do enjoy being with them also. We have done our work. We did our work in different ways and we are in different places. Each human being must find his personal way to his own truths. And when two such people partner up, it is truly a blessed union of two souls.

Speaking of such, ALL souls are connected! That is why when a person who is on his own existential path comes in contact with another such person, she/he just knows and feels that connection. In my lifetime, obviously Martin Luther King,Jr. had it. Bobby Kennedy was just about there when he was cut down. I have met and am dear friends with some others. All of them are gentle and confident and highly spiritual beings. They are serene people. We are connected and we know and feel this.

So, when I am out and about, I am relaxed and comfortable in my own skin. I like people, almost all people, and they can immediately sense this and they relax their mask and begin to let me in. I work very hard to avoid judging any other person. I do, however, disapprove of the way certain people make their choices and of their motives. But they must own their decisions, not I. I take responsibility only for mine. Now, some may consider my comments as being arrogant. Quite the opposite. These are comments made in humility and with gratitude. For, I really have grown way beyond needing, seeking or requiring the acceptance of others. I do not need the approval of a parent, spouse, friend, child, sibling, boss, employer, or government.

I just seek the approval of my God. And I know I have that approval because of the manner in which HE guides me to live my life. Every single decision I have made in my life, positive and negative, has grown me and guided me to be the person I am today. I regret some transgressions, but these were totally unintended and enacted with no malice. They just happened due to the environment, situation and circumstance of the time, and I learned from them all.

ESSAY 67:
Inequities in Life

Let's just restate it...Life is not fair. Life just...is. So to survive it with your physical and mental health, you just have to not take it too seriously. It is all so very temporary. You have to round it off and focus on the positives and do not spend too much time anguishing over the negatives. Negatives always have existed and always will. That is part of the test, the test of living a life. To be alive is to confront one's struggles. Survivors do their best and keep moving forward. Casualties of life do so many things that do not help their cause. They get unduly angered and allow that anger to control and possibly eventually destroy them. They chose to be victims. They seek escape through drugs, alcohol, affairs, working too hard, overeating, electronic media, etc.

In my present case, I became aware that by returning to work part-time after being retired several years, I am now being taxed again on Social Security benefits that were taxes initially to eventually become my benefits when I retired! So, I am being double taxed, screwed by the government, again. So yes, I am upset about this. I know this is not fair, for I am being penalized by returning to the workforce, but what can be done? Nothing! I imagine an underlying reason for this action is to discourage older people from returning to work and take jobs from the younger workers. So, I must reframe this and move forward.

I am blessed that I can still contribute to helping my fellow man by the services I can still provide at my age of 75 years. I am fortunate

I still have the desire and knowledge and skills to continue to make a difference. I am still living a meaningful and rewarding life and many people benefit by my being willing and capable and able to do these things.

I have, for me, a needed work-play balance. This enriches me daily. I have some extra income that permits me to do things that could be somewhat challenging without that added revenue source. I am trying to build some cushion for my estate so my grandchildren can have a better chance to go to college. So, rather than lament all the unfairness, I am aware of it but it does not destroy my day. It does not taint my thinking or motivation. I can release it so it has zero control over me. I am grateful for what I do have and what I can still do and I thank God every day for what circumstances exist in my life. I have so much that so many do not have and I have enough, for me. And I have peace. Priceless!

ESSAY 68:
Soul as Vibrational Energy

The soul of each person has its own frequency, some higher and some lower than others. A rock vibrates at a lower frequency than an amoeba perhaps. Not much going on in a dormant rock, depending on the type of rock. I suspect volcanic rock is higher than sandstone maybe? Some forms just do not have very much vibration going on. Same with people. Some have very high energy vibrational frequencies and some just do not. One can sense this in different people almost immediately.

So, in the "evolution or development or progression" of the soul, each incarnation either on Earth or elsewhere is meant to offer learning opportunities so that one can "climb the ladder of evolution to a higher spiritual level". The goal is to grow and develop and function at a higher frequency with each opportunity given throughout eternity. To raise one's awareness and consciousness with each experienced event. To become more solid and centered and aware of all that IS. To believe most strongly in the divine order of every single thing that exists or has ever existed or will ever exist. Yet knowing that all is ONE with no time qualifier at all.

ESSAY 69:

Raptors, Animals and Humans

As I watch everything from my back patio overlooking the river below on June 1, 2018 I observe our eagle flying low over our yard looking for dinner for her young. The small birds eat seeds. The larger birds, i.e., hawks, eat the smaller ones and small serpents and rodents. The larger eagles eat about anything they can carry off. The thing is, these life forms eat only so they can survive. They do not need to "accumulate wealth" per se. However, chipmunks and squirrels do put a "stash away" but just to provide for themselves and family.

So how is man different? He is different in that once he gets his basic needs met, he gets that disease of MORE. So, rather than have enough to get by, he must take his share and everybody else's also. So anyone and everyone is a potential victim of his desire to get it all for himself. So, which life form is more in tune with God and nature? Which one is more balanced and adhering to the way God set everything up? Which one will endure?

The problem and real test that God granted man in His creating him is he gave man free choice! Of course the test of one's soul is what do you do with your choices? Do you endeavor to get just enough and do so with harmony and integrity and thus progressing to a higher level on your spiritual journey? Or do you victimize others and destroy and just keep "taking from" your entire life?

So basically, Man is not unlike other life forms in that the strong overcome the weak. Thus the stronger ones "rule and dominate "the weaker ones. It is a basic law of nature just as gravity is a basic law. So life being "fair" will never happen. It cannot be. That is why the spiritual path is the only answer. There simply must be a much higher and lasting reason for the existence of all life forms. All life is temporary. It is brief. The only lasting reason for all of it is spiritual. It is the only answer that makes any sense to my beliefs and thinking. The Native Americans believe that life on Earth is the temporary illusion. The spirit life is the real life, for it is never ending. I couldn't agree more!

How else can all these horrible things that man does to his fellow man be explained? The answer for me is that we must all answer to God. That is the end result of our creation in the first place. There simply must be tests, in return for this supreme gift of life we receive. Do we ascend or do we languish and just disappear with our life having zero purpose or meaning? It is up to us to give purpose and meaning to our lives. If we fail to do so, we fail in ways man is not capable of comprehending on a spiritual and cosmic level. What a marvelous experience and journey we can create for ourselves, or not. Freedom of choice.

ESSAY 70:

"Saved" by Jesus Christ!

I have been extremely disappointed and somewhat surprised by the actions of many "born again Christians" as any other group. They claim that to be saved, you must accept Jesus Christ as your Lord and Savior. Fair enough. But really, my truth is that the only person who can save you is you! By that I mean you and your beliefs and behaviors and actions and morality are the only way you can be saved. Many of these people arrogantly believe they can take a short-cut removed from the reality of their lives and simply state the fact that they accept Jesus and that proclamation alone assures their place in heaven. I am sorry. I do not believe that is the way it works! You have to live it, not just say it!

To my thinking, that is nothing but man made doctrine to justify all the inhumane behaviors perpetrated upon others in the name of God and religion. It is just not true! However, there are far too many non-thinking people out there who are truly lost. They need something to believe in, something to hang their hat on. Some sort of "directions", blueprint, or roadmap for which to believe in and obediently follow for a supposed moral life and a guaranteed life everlasting. They seek the easy comfort and security of group think. They are easily led and willingly blindly follow. Many mean well but too many wars have been fought in the name of a God for a specified agenda by a specific religion with their own objectives in mind. Almost always, these goals are based on divisiveness, control, oppression, power, and money.

My opinion is it is not one's spoken beliefs that leads to life ever after. It is one's core beliefs followed by specific and consistent behaviors and actions and morality in all one's treatment of every living creature on this planet! It is trust, conviction, acceptance, tolerance, purity of heart based on love for all, that leads to a life well-lived based on rock solid core principles of right and wrong.

Another observation about Saved Christians is that one must accept Jesus in order to gain entrance into Heaven. Does that mean that the Dali Lama, Gandhi, and other exemplary "non-believers" are denied life ever-after? Really?! Again, the arrogance and agendas of specific religious beliefs is a major root of all true evil perpetrated against one another in the name of "God". The problem is whose God? We are continuing to destroy mankind in the name of religion. It must stop! It is insane and entirely a man made disaster. God must be looking down and just be shaking His head. Stupid, ignorant, insecure humans will do us all in.

ESSAY 71:
Evil vs. Good

I really do believe in my heart of hearts that the forces of good in human beings are much more numerous and natural than the forces of evil. The vast majority of people just want to have someone to love and for someone to love them. They want to have some good friends, a loving and caring family, freedom, live a life with some meaning, be able to provide adequately for themselves and their families. They want to have dignity and respect for themselves and for others. They do not seek domination or control. They simply want peace and peace of mind.

The problem is that the people who view life in this manner are exploited and victimized by the minority. The minority have their values "bass ackwards". They are insecure and seek value and sense of self via controlling and dominating others. They are not spiritual and could care less about other people except in how to use them to dupe or control them to serve their needs. Thus, they take control over the vast majority because the majority are not naturally wired to think this way. They just do not recognize the scheme until it has advanced way beyond a simple solution. They keep wanting to believe that what is happening to them will have a happy ending and everything will be OK. But, it will not be OK soon enough.

The circumstance we are facing as a human race is that the few have most of the power over the many. The trusting, the naive, the followers, the innocent can no longer afford to remain so. We must wake up and join forces and make our stand against all these special interests. We are surrendering what few freedoms we have remaining and it is being done so with our permission.

ESSAY 72:
Blaming the victims!

The powers that be in our society have all the tools to make the laws, try the cases, set up the circumstances whereby the dis-enfranchised have absolutely nothing more to lose by fighting back. The powers refer to it as striking out. Lawbreakers, hooligans, vigilantes, trouble-makers, etc, etc. Thus the powers aim to "clamp down" on all this lawlessness, bring the "rule of law" down upon these undesirable elements!

The fact is that the "authorities" create the very conditions that literally force people of character and integrity to take a stand, and sometimes it is their last stand. No matter, it always has a steep cost to them! These brave individuals are heros to me. Bradley/Chelsea Manning is such an individual. She exposed the government lies about the way we are fighting these wars and the actual consequences to real and innocent victims. The perpetrators were laughing as they fired upon vehicles that proved to contain innocent families with children and then blamed these victims for driving with children in a war zone! Thus, it was the victim's fault!

Yet another police officer was found not guilty of shooting an unarmed black man with his young child in the back seat of his car and his girlfriend taping the episode when she tried to explain that the man was reaching into the glove compartment to retrieve his ID and proof of insurance, etc and NOT reaching for a gun! He was shot anyway! Then when angry blacks demonstrate for the injustice of it all, they are blamed for their "unlawful" behavior! Black Lives Matter is labeled an extremist group!

The Glenwall fire in London was due to the fact that numerous safety regulations were repeatedly ignored, despite years of complaints from the tenants, who are now dead! No sprinkler system in the 24 story housing complex. Inadequate construction with cheaper non-fire retardant materials. No fire escapes. Inadequate fire alarms, numerous safety violations that were reported but swept under the rug. All this occurred under the last three administrations of Tory Party rule. Now PM May is being held accountable, as she should. The Labor Party demands changes! PM May did a George Bush with Katrina. No comprehension, no understanding, no empathy, no facing the victims. A cowardly act by one who accepts zero responsibility.

Victims become victims as the eventual result brought about by the direct actions of those in power. People who want to work, find no jobs available. Jobs are sent overseas so big business can line their pockets at society's expense! Poverty wages, zero benefits, no government or environmental oversight or protections. With no ability to find work, a person starts to lose his self-esteem. He feels he is inadequate. Cannot support his family. Eventually, he will likely seek some sort of escape mechanism via drugs, sex, booze, crime, etc. All these possible choices are bad for society. So, power creates these circumstances that spawn these situations that result in these anti-society problems with very predictable results. So power labels these people "losers", for in doing so they can claim that these people made certain choices and thus, by laws of a "civilized "society, they must pay the price.

I can truly understand that man from the Midwest who has just had it with politicians! He especially blames the party of Trump for so much social injustice and growing inequality in this country. And rightfully so, but Democrats are tainted also. So he shot a congressman at their annual softball game and it cost him his life. He just needed to make his statement and he did. There will be more of this because people are completely disgusted with the stacked deck against them! Violence will continue to escalate because people can find no other way to express their frustration and rage. Anger begets more anger. He was a Sanders supporter and Sanders was victimized also, by the DNC! Everything that happens to people has an effect on their lives and all these actions by power have reactions eventually, and consequences.

And so many of the rich and powerful have very little or no social conscience at all. They state that they should not "bail out" all the "losers" by giving any of their money to help these types of people. It is their "own hard earned money" and they have no intention of giving any of it away. Not to the government either, for they will waste it too!

ESSAY 73:

Lessons from Bees

Our country could learn all they need about world affairs by observing the behavior of bees. Bees build their "cities" ie. hives in their preferred and hopefully safe and secure locations. They just want to take care of their own little corner of the world and not be disturbed by others. They could care less how others live or what they do. However, when an uninvited entity enters their domain, they will do as every species does. They will be on alert and defend their territory if they feel threatened.

So, if a human gets too close, they are very cautious as they watch the behavior of the human. When the human enters their domain and for example, decides they want to touch the nest, then a few bees will attack! If the human tries to steal their honey or strikes the nest with a stick, the bees will swarm them with all force available. Their very existence, their way of life is being directly threatened! They will all be willing to die to protect the survival of the hive. And a single bee will sting a hugely larger human knowing that to release their stinger will kill them as it will, potentially, the man.

The radical segments of Islam, in my opinion, did not originally intend to destroy western civilization. But, our actions in their countries have led to the very creation of this enemy against us! We caused them! We go all over the world taking what we want from lesser countries because we have the power to do so! We disrupt their societies, we steal their resources, we support their oppressive dictators, we threaten their cultures, we try to impose our values on them, etc, etc. These ancient societies just wanted to be left alone, and do as they always have done. We have no moral or legal right to rape them as we have!

So, what can these small powerless countries and peoples do? We are stronger but they fight us in any way they can. They radicalize because their puppet governments permit these actions by us against their own people! We own their leaders and the citizens be damned. We promote the lie that these people are jealous of our way of life, our "freedoms" and want to destroy us. We "sell" this lie to testosterone ripe young males who want to "protect" their country. Also to uninformed and non-thinking masses who just play follow the leader all their lives! The fact is they are seduced by their government to protect our country's special interests, or American interests, as they state it to the masses. Be a patriot and support the American way of life! Anyone who dares question or dissents is a traitor. What a croc! Wake up citizens! It is a total con job!

ESSAY 74:

"Serving" my Country

What does that mean, really? It is a phrase used by the government in which it demands and expects its current generation of young adults to pay their dues and serve and protect our country. However, what are we really protecting and who are we actually serving? We are actually protecting the "interests"of the powers that be in our country. We are allowing the entrenched special interests of this country to continue their strangleholds on all the populace who they need to insure their place of power.

They use that emotional word "patriotism" to hook our emotions and subvert them to

be used for entirely wrong and misleading purposes. The military-industrial complex Eisenhower warned about in the 1950's is thriving and very much alive and well. We are always more than ready to find a just cause for a war that we can sell to the American people. Thus, our politicians enrich their friends in the defense industry and our military leaders get to seek out their glory and get their promotions and test out and use all the latest toys of destruction.

Lots of profits are generated at taxpayer expense to fund these adventures. Another glaring example of redistribution of wealth from the have-nots to the haves. Our leaders get to use all the propaganda at their disposal to entice these young people to fight the newest war.

And if these people refuse, they are labeled as traitors to their country and imprisoned or punished in all sorts of ways.

I must ask, "What right does a government (just people like us who have more power) have, to expect a person who has his own value system as a human being to surrender his moral beliefs to a group of people who have an agenda that is totally and absolutely against what we believe to be right, moral and just?" How can one permit this to happen and still be able to live with himself as he is going against what he believes in his soul to be so unjust and wrong? To go along with this is to surrender your soul to a lesser being or to a corrupt government.

It takes a huge amount of courage to say "no" when your government demands you do certain things you know are morally wrong. They would state that you owe this to your country. A price you must pay. You live here, you owe a debt. To whom? You were fortunate enough to have been born here, just as your leaders were. You are a good citizen, you pay your taxes, you vote, you work hard and honestly, you contribute to the economy and your community, you take nothing and are a burden on no one. What more do you owe?

Are these "leaders" of strong enough conviction that they would willingly give their lives for this "just" cause? Only persons of strong moral convictions will reject this demand of the government. These wars and the reasons for fighting them have to be exposed. People have to start thinking for themselves and speak out against this continuous con job. It just never ends! The same argument has been used by governments for millennia. We just have to wise up.

However, there is a class of human beings that just enjoy war. They are the warrior class and it seems to be in their DNA. They will always exist. Let them kill each other. Just count me out for I see the absurdity of all this senseless mayhem. BTW, I am a veteran of the Vietnam War. I joined during the Tet Offensive and I lost eight friends there. What a waste of resources and life that was!

The government is so cunning. They promote the "team" concept and "manhood" to these young and naive kids in high school. One of love of country, glory, honor, duty, etc. all emotional concepts that sell to these young people. Then they brainwash and re-program them to be heartless killers. Then they turn them loose all over the world to do their bidding. Quite a con game they have going.

And the lack of opportunity these kids have due to inferior education, poor economic outlooks, no skills, leads them to serve their "masters." They join up, for the oppressive system that creates these circumstances for these kids gives them few choices. Thus, the capitalists and industrialists and imperialists who create and perpetuate this system of inequity continually benefit from it. Perfect for them. And the beat goes on, and on, and on.

ESSAY 75:

Taxes, IRS, Humanity

I could choose to complain and be very angry at the "penalties" i.e. unjust taxes that most everyday Americans are required to pay! For what? Where is the value of these taxes? However, to obsess over this is a form of surrender to the government for I am permitting them to control me, my thinking. So, I shall focus on the fact I do reside in a country where things could be much worse! I am on my way out. I can still make a contribution to my fellow man. I am currently able to pay these unjust taxes. So, I will just have to pay them in order to continue to live my life by the moral principles I have always sought to follow. Money has never been my primary goal in life. So, I "donate "to live.

I am fortunate I have the means to pay off these morally bankrupt thieves! It allows me to focus on more important things that really matter in my life. Of course, life is not fair! People seek power to dominate others. It has always been so and will continue till the end. So, I pay my price, my dues, to stay involved in my life. I can still do some good. I choose to focus on the just and good deeds, rather than obsess over all the injustice in this present world we all occupy. I could be in a far more dire circumstance. These taxes are a burden but it is more an inconvenience that I must resolve than an obstacle I have no means to overcome.

ESSAY 76:
Religions

The USA was founded as a Christian nation. Catholics and Protestants. Now we have the Jewish influence and the Muslim factions, et al. Historically forever, even among just the Protestants, we have always fought, judged, condemned, attempted to destroy those with different ways to believe in God. The Crusades were horrific, and fought in the name of God, my God vs. your God, for Pete's sake! Now with Muslim influence growing all over the world, we are at war with each other everywhere. Their God was represented by Mohammed and ours by Jesus. Theirs was founded by their beliefs and ours by the love of Jesus, the "son" of God, who was destroyed in body by his oppressors. There are always oppressors. The insecure people who seek to destroy those perceived to be threats to their position of power and need for domination over others.

And today, nothing has changed. New oppressors, new victims, new targets, ad nauseum. We will never destroy ISIS, because it is a cancerous ideology and the powerless have zero to lose. To give up their lives is an honor for they are disenfranchised in this present life anyway. How could death be worse than what they are now experiencing? And there will always be lost souls on this earth, be they ISIS or whatever future name they will be called. The fact is that people just have never gotten along, except when they have mutually beneficial reasons to do so, and that is always temporary.

War has always existed and the weapons that exist today will eliminate man from the equation sooner rather than later. I have written of this before. The main point is that religion has divided us since the very beginning and it will always do so. We just are not capable as human beings, of going beyond a specific religion and seeing the totality of "Oneness" we all share with everything! Very sad but the only conclusion that I can reach. Truly though, God's will be done and I am but a dust speck so I can certainly accept this scenario if that is God's will. However, God will not destroy man, man is most capable of doing this all by himself, thank you.

God will allow this to happen because He sees and knows all and when man is supposed to disappear, he will do so. Everything is forever, no beginning and no end. Man's very existence and "rule" is a micro-blink in forever! A planet is formed somewhere in the universe. Eventually, species may originate on that planet, they evolve, they then gradually or suddenly disappear for all kinds of reasons. It goes on for all eternity. That is the cosmic "joke"! In the huge scheme of things, puny mankind does not matter one iota. We are deliberate accidents of cosmic dust. We "control" nothing! Period! Get over ourselves!

I know, a cynical outlook, but it is what I have observed from way, way above. Calling it the way I see it. At least I have given much thought to this. Trying to find the answers-for me. So, why are we even here? To be tested and to test ourselves. To grow, develop and evolve. To attempt to reach our potential. To appreciate. To trust, surrender, and to accept. To love.

ESSAY 77:

Working, in retirement years...The Gift!

I am learning what I had hoped to be learning at my age of 74 now. I retired at age 65, 10 months. Thus, I collect full Social Security. After many years of no set schedule and more than enough "free time" spent pursuing things I wanted to pursue while still young enough and healthy enough to do so, I am still excited by new life lessons. When I work for several days and then have several days off after working, I am liking where my life is. I am so pleased that I still really have a genuine passion for my chosen dental profession. I am so very blessed and fortunate that I have made myself very valuable to a Medicaid Clinic that sorely needs my services. I love the stimulation of problem solving with the many clinical situations I am presented with.

Thus, to my point. How can a person who continues to give a damn and has certain learned skills that are still in demand ever be fulfilled by just existing and being in a leisure state of fun and games all the time? What is stimulating about constant leisure? Where does growth occur? What can challenge you? What is your contribution to your fellow man? How can one fend off boredom and lethargy? I have always believed that as long as I am able and have the desire, I should be doing "something" that is productive in some way.

The more a person just sits around, the harder it becomes to avoid doing just that! I am so excited to still be able to work, but on MY terms at this age. I decide when and where and how much I want to work. I have zero work worries. No employees, no mortgage or rent, no bank loans, no overhead, no management decisions, no equipment repairs, no employee concerns, etc. No headaches and no responsibilities except doing a decent job at the chair while taking care of my patients. I am an employee, rather than an employer, for the first time in my long career. It frees me from all the headaches and responsibilities from running my own practice, so I may just do what I truly enjoy, treat dental patients, period!

So the beauty is, when I have worked a couple days, I am then off for several days. When my work obligations are over, I find myself feeling newly liberated, in that I now have some free time that I want to take advantage of. Remember that "Schools Out" feeling? I get that every week! This "concept" still excites me! Thus, rather than being bored by just another day like the last, I am pumped up that my time is now totally mine and I look forward to spending my energy doing all these things I could not do because I was working!

Thus, we can use our more compressed leisure moments to spend time socializing, playing tennis, pickleball, swimming, running errands, traveling, doing "stuff" etc. The point being, having less "free time" motivates me to do lots of different things during those moments. Thus, when it all gets done, I am ready to work a bit again. So, having some regular work to do condenses my life in that the leisure time is more limited, thus stimulating me to use that play time more wisely and productively. It becomes more cherished and savored, rather than taken for granted, as can occur when all days are leisure days of sameness.

For me, productive work is necessary for my soul. But, I now have achieved, as was my desire, the balance that comes from some work and some play. And the work is elective, not necessary to work to survive, which puts a whole new frame of reference on work. When one has to work vs. when one wants to work, what a difference that makes in a healthy attitude toward living a good and satisfying life. There is a huge difference between working at something you have no passion for just to pay the bills and working at something you truly love just because you have the desire to do so!

For me, it is all about the quality of one's life. Life is more than simply sucking air till your final gasp. Life is to be seized and celebrated! It is all about passion, preparation, commitment, performance, effort, contribution, and belief. Anything short of this in my mind is a life just taken for granted and not wisely and productively lived. The statement "I didn't ask to be born" is something that has always bothered me. To utter this tells me that this sacred gift was not truly appreciated by the recipient and thus had not the value to that receiver to be worth the effort to make that opportunity all that it could have been. "Poor me "has never cut it to my frame of mind. A "victim" because you were born? How sad an attitude is that?!? I have no space in my life for people such as this.

To conclude, I am so thankful I can still make a difference in some people's lives, and I remain healthy enough in mind and body and spirit to be able to continue to be able to observe, learn, grow, and contribute to others in some way that also facilitates my own growth as the years increasingly slide by. My goal is to experience, grow and learn as long as I can breathe. And at the end, sigh and smile a little grin and say "Thank You my dear Lord! "I tried, as much as possible for me, to do my best. And any potential moisture or tear will not be one of sadness, but one of trust, love, gratitude, and appreciation! "Onward" I am ready! Let's do this! For I am, as before, now, always and forever... ONE! What else is there to say?

ESSAY 78:
Removing the Surface Crust

I have found that at times it can be difficult, yet necessary, to remove that outer layer, that crust we all develop that shields us and to some extent, protects us from all the things we must deal with in living our lives on a daily basis. Sometimes, strenuous exercise helps with this. Endorphin production clears the mind for me.

This society we live in can be so demanding in so many ways. Pressures build up, we must protect ourselves from too much of this from time to time. That is why we exercise, cultivate friendships, socialize, escape in sports, music, travel, dance, get outdoors, shop, etc. Sometimes a bit of alcohol helps to remove the crust or to peel the onion. Doing some of these things when the need is there, may be necessary to keep going.

Whatever the means, we need to have a way to get deeper at times, dare to venture below the surface, and make some sense of it all. We need to release and when we remove the crud of the outer protective layer, we can better get to know our own individual truths. I feel this is a life-long journey. To me, it has to on some level make some sense for me to stay engaged in the game.

I believe that to travel is a wonderful way to remove yourself from the daily grind and routines of your life and expand your horizons and comfort zones. You are never exactly the same person when you return from a trip as you were before you left. You will have changed. You will have learned something new, experienced and seen something you never saw before. You will have grown. Your perspectives may change, points of view evolve. You come to identify with other people in other environments, other cultures, how they live, what they think. This broadens you. Expose yourselves to new experiences. Grow yourself.

ESSAY 79:
Circling the Drain

Anniversary of Pearl Harbor...I saw President Obama's address last night. I agree with his approach re: guns and ISIS. Certain members of Congress 100 % disagree, of course. I am just feeling we learn nothing, ever. They use Pearl Harbor as an excuse to go to war again. Always go to war. More guns, more violence, more reasons to kill, to dominate, to impose our will over theirs, and vise-versa.

So, I have again concluded, we, as a world civilization, will always want to kill each other and justify our position and reasoning to do so. We are right and they are wrong. We are good and they are bad. We will show them who's boss. No harmony exists and divisiveness is getting worse than ever. It is everywhere. Nature is a harmonious state. It seeks to maintain an equilibrium. Ebb and flow. Natural cycles. Seasons flow evenly from one to the next. The circle of life for all on this planet. It is a natural rule of law that has always been so.

Man has been interfering for eons and it has accelerated to a pace and on a scale that is not sustainable and is on the very cusp of irreversible. In fact, I do believe the tipping point is past. Look all around you. Climate is fighting back to seek equilibrium against what damage man has imposed on our natural cycles. War is everywhere. Hate is epidemic. Fear is replacing reason. Economic collapse is imminent. Inequality is worse than ever before. We, as human beings and as a species, are truly circling the drain and all one can do, on an individual basis, is to make every attempt to live right with oneself and with God.

That does NOT mean to follow organized religion per se. Religion does have its place for many people. However, each religion has their own self-serving agenda. To live right with God DOES mean to live a spiritual and meaningful life with conviction, passion. effort, appreciation, love, tolerance, humility, awareness, and gratitude. Just strive to reach an awareness to realize the actual TRUTH! The truth of you and the gift of life. The trust in God that He is the only answer, for He is...the only answer! Man, in his arrogance, is destroying everything. Only you can save yourself from these ravages by trusting and surrendering to the will of God.

NOTE...I do not intend to sound preachy here. This is not a sermon. But, I can see where it can be interpreted that way. All I am trying to say is that man has made such an abysmal mess of everything that the ONLY way to make any sense of all this is to let go of the illusion of man as being the "answer" to these problems. Man creates these problems and his "solutions "create bigger problems! So, drop out of this thinking. Go with what always has been perfect and always shall be perfect. Go with God's Law; discount and dismiss the law of man. That is the only way to find true peace and contentment in this human existence on the planet Earth, as it exists today. Seek harmony within yourself for that is the only true and lasting place it can be found.

Everything in nature was in harmony, as a system, before man. The entire universe has been, is and always will be in harmony. Man is but a tiny blip and he is disharmony to the system. By nature's law, what is in disharmony must eventually be eliminated from the system to allow the system to self-correct. As I am seeing this, man is in disharmony and he will be eliminated from the system. The difference is that man will not need an outside source to destroy it. Man is so capable of doing this all by itself. As stated, we are now circling the drain. Sad, tragic, but to my eyes, true. It seems to be what it seems to be.

ESSAY 80:
Trade Agreements Ruse, and "HOPE?"

Under the Bill Clinton presidential terms, there was a great sales pitch to the American people about the need and benefits of international free trade agreements. NAFTA with Mexico was the first. He said that it would open up the markets for American goods overseas. Ross Perot stated that what Americans would hear would be a "giant sucking sound" of American jobs going south of the border. He was 100% correct! And we all knew that would be the case. What it actually did was give American business an escape from cumbersome environmental regulations, saved tens of millions of dollars in labor costs and pension plan and health care funding requirements.

So rather than "help" the American worker, it hurt him and further enriched these re-located businesses. Not only that, these corporations did not pay taxes on monies made overseas! What a sweet deal for them! So, the citizens were grossly misled. To "sell" this concept to the people, a narrative was required, of course. So Congress and these special interests emphasized the "perceived benefits" to the reluctant and skeptical American populace. Lower consumer prices from goods made overseas and sold in America. New markets for American goods. They mentioned nothing about the windfalls they would be reaping at the taxpayers expense!

My wife and I, in our travels, have seen first hand examples of the work camps in Mexico that produce all these products that used to be made in America. They are abysmal working and living environments that take advantage of oppressed and disadvantaged people who will work under any conditions just to barely survive. The USA condones this by doing the bidding for these companies that keep these legislators in power. How morally and ethically bankrupt we are as a country to encourage and support this!

In this regard, Hillary deserved to lose. She intended to do more of the same. Trump says he will punish these companies. I hope he does because if that happens, I will cut him a bit more slack. The jury is certainly out but I am hoping he accomplishes this above all else. These companies need to be paying their fair share and become, again, pillars of their local communities. We need to start rebuilding our middle class. We need to be creating new jobs by bringing manufacturing back again to America. Clean manufacturing, not polluting ones of old. Clean energy jobs, not fossil fuels. I will be watching what happens there with Trump also.

A conclusion from this is that one must ALWAYS look HARD under the surface, for there is always another more sinister and hidden agenda for those pushing a particular concept so hard. Become a probing skeptic, always! The harder they push, the deeper I look. What is THEIR benefit in this? What is the REAL cost to us? How will this look in five years, ten years? What has the effect been? We know what the effect has been with these trade agreements. They have decimated the working class. We cannot survive or thrive as a nation with no middle class. The economic and social structures will all break down, as they are now. We are on the very cusp of early anarchy if things do not change for the better under Trump. The people have spoken, so we shall see.

A key question I have for a supreme narcissist is this. If one wants to become beloved and adored and adulated by the masses, why would you act in ways to alienate much of the population? Why not do the right thing, down the line, to satisfy the masses, rather than the top elites of the country? Why not be a Lincoln, who is canonized, rather than a Nixon? Be transformative in a good way! Trump has an opportunity to be truly great and it seems an egomaniac such as he is smart enough to see this opportunity to make a real difference in America and this world.

He claims he is a master negotiator and deal maker and I imagine he has some skills in this area. One principle of making a good deal is to not let the opposition know what you are thinking and your real position or bottom line. I am sensing that he is making all these outlandish statements and taking such extreme positions so he can have room to maneuver. He can back off, as he has done in some instances already and then give the impression that he is listening and willing to change or compromise his former position. Thus, he gets the deal he had in mind in the first place. He claims to be a master at this tactic. To him, it seems this has always been a game and he claims he has become very, very skilled at it. Time will tell.

The chess match between him and all these special interests, and these career politicians, and the electorate with their expectations will be the ultimate dance for him. In many ways, he has spent his entire life preparing for this opportunity. And at age 70 he will be fighting his last and greatest battle and he knows this and my hope is he is more than willing and very ready. I did sense that he gained some empathy for the downtrodden people of this country as he was campaigning across the rust belt of America. These people live in a world that he knew nothing about. I felt he identified more with them than the fat cats he has surrounded himself with his entire life. But he could be playing and using them too. If he does not seize this opportunity to be truly great, he is much dumber than I believe him to be. We shall see.

He has played the press, the Republican Party, and the electorate to varying degrees. Is he playing Putin? (Putin is playing him!) Is he playing Congress? Or, is he playing himself?!?! Very curious to find out. Time will reveal the answer soon enough. I am sorry, but I am very skeptical that he is capable of serving anyone but himself and those in his close inner circle. It has worked for him his entire life so what incentive would he have to change and what skills has he nurtured to be capable of really caring about the "little people"? To be transformative, he must first transform himself and at age 70, that is no small endeavor.

ESSAY 81:
Less is MORE

It is my belief that one should not get all they "desire". One should grow to the point that they learn to desire less and then, in reality they actually have more. People who constantly seek more never stop in their quest. It can slowly but steadily develop into the progressive disease of MORE. It can become a lifelong pattern of living, in that one is never actually living in, and enjoying the present moment. They are always looking into the future for the next "thing" or whatever. By always living in the future, they forgo the present, which is all one really has ie. this present moment.

The reason you have "more", is what you have in this moment is "enough." So if you have enough, why do you need more? Wanting more, and all the time, energy and resources required to achieve this, is an insidious disease and a thief of lives. It affects people, business, governments, nations. One must learn the difference between "wanting" something and "needing" something. To need something to make your life better or easier is a worthy goal and worth spending time and effort to attain. To simply want it and just attain it for that reason alone is foolish and potentially addictive behavior that can get you in economic trouble eventually.

It can also clutter your life and complicate it in that it becomes another possession you must take care of, create room for and continually try to justify. Just a waste all the way around. However, it is important to give yourself permission to treat and reward yourself from time to time. If a recent purchase serves this purpose and does not become habitual behavior of simply impulsive buying, then go for it. Gotta do some "feel good stuff" once in a while!

Also, notice that people who finally got that "raise" they always wanted, that new car, that boat, that house, that vacation of a lifetime, soon become bored and want something else. The reason they want something else is because they have that emptiness inside that tells them that if "this" happens, then all will be good for them and all is well in their lives. That empty hole will be filled. Until it isn't. However, if one can truly appreciate what they have in this present moment, no more is needed to remain happy. We all know that true happiness must come from within, not from the outside. Of course, it is desirable to seek improvements in one's situation. That desire is necessary for stimulation and growth. But that desire should be something that one seeks out of need, rather than just pure want.

People who have most "everything", in reality, are frequently bankrupt as human beings. They mortgage their lives in the present for an uncertain future. They often have unhappy failed marriages, spoiled, wasteful, lazy, and unappreciative children, few close trusted friends, and resentful and envious people in their circles. They tend to abuse alcohol, do drugs, work far too much, have affairs, health problems, etc. They just become lost souls who never had a clue about the truly important lessons of a life lived with meaning and purpose. And people who lose their souls can become very dangerous people to themselves and to others whose lives they touch and impact along the way.

As a country, I can sadly state that America has lost its soul and it has done so for all the reasons stated above. I can get more into that as a potential future topic. Thus, I obviously conclude, as I always have maintained, that one's soul is one's very own personal soul and that is all one can be truly expected to nurture, develop and grow on our micro-blink flicker on this planet called Earth.

ESSAY 82:

Lending Money to Family and Friends, A sticky wicket

When/if you loan money to your children, do it and do not expect to be repaid. For whatever reason, many children just assume you have "lots of money" and do not really need it. At least, you don't need it as much as they do, to their eyes. For me, it is a bit of a character test just to see if they will at least offer or make an effort to repay the "loan" in toto or in part. For some reason to them, a loan seems to mean a gift.

When asked to loan money to a friend, it can change the relationship. The potential loaner may resent being asked for that places them in an uncomfortable position. If they refuse to loan the money, the friendship can be severely strained. If they do loan the money, they may think less of the requester for getting into the situation of needing money from you. Why not go to a bank? Why not sell something? Why not get an extra job? Why not be smarter? Why not be more careful? Why were you so foolish? All these questions can arise. And if you loan the money and if the loan is very slow being repaid or not repaid, the friendship will likely be over.

Thus, not a good idea. A lose-lose. Rather, brainstorm with the requester on other possible ways you can help them get out of their predicament. Or try to be a friend in some other way. Just explain to them that you really value the friendship and do not want to risk straining it or losing it over money. Inform them that your policy, gained from past experience, is to not lend money to friends. I hope you can respect that. Be firm and consistent in your position. If they do not respect your decision, the friendship was not as valuable to them as it was to you. So, you get your learnings and move on with some gained wisdom and insights about this person.

ESSAY 83:

In Decline

As one enters middle age, most people become aware that they are in decline in certain individual capacities. It may be physical, mental or a combination or both. Some are in more decline than others for all sorts of reasons. That is a fact of the human life cycle. I am well aware that I do not have the energy or ambition that I once had. My body cannot do what it used to do and my mind does not even want it to. Today, at age 74, to do a single significant task requiring some effort is all I usually aim to achieve in a single day. I attempt to do something of value on a daily basis. I make an attempt to do some physical exertion most days. Just make an effort to do something each day! That something includes some moments for just me. To think, to plan, to be in the moment with something I want to do. The goal is to stay involved with life in as many varied ways as possible.

At my age, and years younger, we are all in decline. We must accept this as it has always been so. We lose our fizz at different rates and in different areas of mind and body. So I strive to not lament that fact, no "woe is me" thinking. I choose to focus on what I can still do and want to do, rather than what I can no longer do. I am appreciative of what I have done and of what I can still do. I continue to marvel at the phenomenal gift of this thing called life. Even though I am slowing down, I am blessed that I am still living my life, even if it is on the wane. Would I rather curse my circumstance and be done with life, or would I better choose to still be glad I am among the living? I can still think, observe, feel, taste, smell, hear, see, remember, love and be loved, grow, work, learn and participate in certain activities.

Why would I want to be depressed or non-appreciative of what I am still able to do? Yes, I can be sad at my losses. But I still have all those glorious memories of times now confined primarily to my mind. And I still have my thoughts, so I still have me. At this very moment, I am sitting on my river deck and observing and listening to the streaming water. I can hear the birds and the squirrels. I am observing a clear Vermont sky with soft cumulus white clouds overhead. What is it that I am lacking at this very moment? Nothing! If I were destitute, homeless, crippled, hungry, ill-clothed, whatever, I would still have this priceless, valued, and treasured moment! I have it right now and I appreciate right now and I savor and treasure this very point in time. What is life really all about if one cannot create and truly enjoy moments?

I am looking at the river bank below me. There is a photo in our home of my wife's mother's mother when she was 18 years old reading a book in that same area of grass in that very location. She passed on long ago.Her life was lived. Her daughter, Bonnie's mother is several years gone also. Her life was also lived and now past. My wife is 72 years old now. She is closer to her end also. The point is that we are all born, live our life, pass on and so it has always been, for all life forms. It is such a very brief event so no matter what is transpiring in one's life, we must keep it all in perspective.

Yes, we have good moments, great moments, disappointments, failures, accomplishments, losses, pain, suffering and victories too. But above all, as long as we are breathing, we have our life, no matter what we are experiencing in our respective states of decline. So decline is a fact of life, unless we are cut down early by some unexpected and sudden event. To get to decline can be viewed as a gift of sorts, in it's own way. It slows us down so we are more ready and motivated to look within, to develop our spirits as we have spent our entire lives chasing our tails on that treadmill our society calls life. We have more time now to get in touch with what truly matters, if we are so inclined to make the effort to start going deeper within ourselves. For within ourselves is where we can find our answers to what really matters.

God blessed us with life and with our own inner workings that are unique to each living soul. How can we not honor this gift by getting in touch with what has always been within us, at our soul level? To me, we owe it to ourselves, and to our Maker, to make this discovery while we have the opportunity to do so. To be able to achieve this before our bodies desert us is the most noble and necessary thing a human being can do. Only then can one smile at that final breath and say "Thank You" and be able to mean it at the deepest level. You do not just mean it, you truly feel it at your core. You are truly thankful!

We have so much to still learn when we separate the mind from the body. So those among us who depart early, before decline seeps into their lives, are not given this opportunity to discover all this wisdom for the ages. It does require effort to do this and the vast majority of human beings have no idea what I am speaking about and no desire or ability to even conceive of this. They have no concept of even how to take some initial action. This can only be achieved individually. You cannot find any of your answers except from deep within you. These are, of necessity, your answers to your questions.

To my mind, those who are seeking meaning must each attempt to do this and the reward for this is supreme peace of mind, and an ability to not take anything too seriously. Every single thing that happens to us, whether perceived as positive or negative, provides to us an opportunity to learn and grow. We have no power except power over ourselves in that how do we reframe these events and grow from them and how do we choose to handle all the complexities and circumstances of just being alive?

As a person comes to recognize and accept his/her decline, which happens to all of us at different ages and different rates, an interesting thing can happen. If one is receptive to it and comes to cultivate it, when a person starts to distance himself from his bodily circumstance and starts to go within to his spiritual side, he begins a transcendence. He begins to see things from a totally different point of view. He sees through corrected lenses for perhaps the first time. He begins to see events and circumstances more clearly and attaches a different meaning to them than in the past.

Some things that used to seem important become reframed and they do not occupy one's attention, energy, and thought quite so much. Priorities are re-arranged. Clarity becomes known with more certainty and serenity ensues. Wisdom and peace of mind grow in one's awareness and a supreme connection with the correctness of the concept of "ONE". We, as individuals, come to internalize and truly feel this divine connection at the soul level. I have written other essays on my thoughts of the soul, and Divine energy, and to me, I have come to some sense and meaning of it all. I truly feel at peace with my answers, for me.

Is it possible I am "wrong"? Of course it is! Very likely that is the case. But I am not incorrect,for me. Deep thinkers have wrestled with this for millennia. However, as stated before, these are of necessity, my answers for me as each of us must arrive at one's own answers. These make sense to me. They fit with me. I feel very connected to what I truly believe and I am very comfortable with how I perceive the "big picture". I have come to acceptance. And if this is the way I truly feel at the soul level, how can I possibly be "wrong" for I am just putting voice to feelings and beliefs that God placed deep within me.

Only I can possibly know how correct this feels. My hope is that more people learn to sit back and observe closely this absurd dance of life as it exists on this planet. When more of us get deeper, the answers will raise us all to a higher level of awareness and consciousness and life will have more value and meaning for the entire human race. Our choices and perceptions will become less ego-driven and more motivated by love and co-operation and acceptance. As stated in other essays, I have a little hope, but I am not optimistic.

ESSAY 84:

Personal, Extreme Gratitude

It is 3:45 am on Saturday, July 22, 2017. I am just feeling such gratitude for where I am in my life. My circumstances have led me back to a profession that I have loved my entire life. When I was younger, after many decades in dentistry, I went through a period of pseudo burn-out when I was feeling trapped by my situation. I was working too hard and was responsible for far too many people. My former wife had no appreciation for all that I was doing and giving so the family could be "well enough" taken care of. They took me for granted and I started to become resentful and bitter. I also was lamenting the trap that I was in with my large group dental practice. I was tired with no way out. I saw no end to it. Finally, I was able to create the situation by which I could find a way to escape and be free of all that responsibility.

I knew I needed to leave the city and state I had spent my professional career in. It was time. I was so finished with everything it represented. I needed to create a new circumstance in my life. My current wife and I wanted to travel and meet new and stimulating people and see and do new things we enjoyed. And we did this for over 7 years, in retirement. My unmet financial goals, in that I wanted to be able to help our five grandchildren be able to have a college education, if they desired, forced me to really examine where I was in my life at age 72. I was becoming lethargic, less motivated, and a bit bored and restless with my daily, weekly, and monthly routines. I felt out of balance. I was missing dentistry and I needed to remind myself of all the reasons I became a dentist. So, I carefully processed all these facts of my life at that time.

We needed to generate some income in order to meet our goal of being able to help our grandchildren, if needed. A dear and special friend pointed out a community clinic to me and lamented how no local dentists treated Medicaid patients. I was led to investigate that facility. The flow became that I was able to observe their operation and thus think long and hard. Do I really want to do this again? Do I still have the capabilities? Can I get up to speed with all the new materials and procedures? Will I enjoy this again? Do I want to jump thru all the necessary hoops to get my dental license in another state? Will I pull the trigger or bail out? I did pull that trigger. It was not an easy process.

It took one year to obtain my new license. I was hired by that clinic to provide dental services to the underserved and to Medicare patients. To my great relief, my dormant skills soon reached full bloom. It was as if I never left! My passion returned. Now that I am back in this profession that I really do love, I am finding that I am still able to truly help people. My skills are as good as ever. My surgical expertise is still excellent. My comfort zone and learning curve has expanded to cover everything I do clinically with skill, confidence, and competence. I am still growing. There is always a way!

So, I can say that my life is vastly enriched on a daily basis by my doing dentistry again. I feel so gratified when providing treatment to these wonderful and interesting people. They stimulate my life. I care about them and they know it. I do not talk down to them. I try to listen carefully and I am careful and compassionate and empathetic to their situation. I try to make their lives better and no matter how tired I can get, it is a very good and satisfying tired. This effort I put forth grows my mind, enriches me and feeds my soul.

By being motivated to get back into dentistry, I thank God for He led me to this place at this time to do these things at this point in my life. He has presented me with the opportunity to recognize what I can still do to aid others and my being able to continue to evolve in so many ways. He has granted me the means to still be capable of taking care of my health, mind, body, and most importantly, my spirit. He allows me to still want to learn new things. So many of my friends over the years have now departed or have serious health issues. They stopped learning and doing years ago. They are now just treading water till their end. I still can "be" and am very fortunate to be able to continue to live an active and stimulating life. I just feel so blessed in all ways possible and I pray I may continue to be able to contribute to others for many more productive years.

I know that my practicing dentistry again, in this new town and at this time is improving the lives of many people in this area. I have stepped up to the plate and am trying to continue to make a small difference in this world. That makes all my efforts worthwhile to me and I know how truly fortunate I am to still have the desire, mind, skills, health and circumstance to do what I still love to be doing. So, from the depth of my heart and soul and with utmost appreciation, I thank you God for the gifts You have given me and I pray that I may continue to be able to serve Your purposes for as long as You deem this to continue to happen. Thank You, so very, very much!!!

ESSAY 85:

Arthur Ashe Book... Meaning of life and lessons and messages

Note... This is a quote from Dr. Howard Thurman as he has written about Arthur Ashe while he was dying "Any tragedy has inherent in it positive good......The pain of life may teach us to understand life, and in doing so, to more fully love, embrace, and appreciate life. To love life truly is to be whole in all one's parts; and thus to be truly free and thus unafraid. There is a quiet courage that comes from an inward spring of confidence in the meaning and significance of life. This courage and understanding is like an underground river, flowing far beneath the surface noise and shifting events of one's life events." Believing that pain has a purpose, I do not question its place in the universe or my (Arthur Ashe) fate in becoming so familiar with pain through disease. Death is but a continuum of life.

JHW addendum..."It (death) is something that occurs IN life rather than TO life. Death is but one of the many occurrences in life. The meaning of the concept of life does not change at the moment of physical death."

ESSAY 86:
Solitude

I grew up in a rural southern state. So, having periods of being alone at varying periods of time shaped me in many ways. With solitude I learned how to sort out my thoughts. It energized me and became part of my circadian rhythm. There have been periods in my life since that childhood that I have been very much missing that alone time. I have found myself seeking opportunities to just think and process. I realized I needed to separate from outside stimuli, noise, mental clutter, people, and just stuff. I am on MY OWN individual spiritual journey, as many people are, and thus it is my quest and this, of necessity, must be a solitary process.

Native Americans, monks, Buddists, etc. have forever recognized this need. They all sought their answers, their true meaning, in solitude. So, in this regard it IS all about me. One must take care of oneself first, in order to be present for the needs of others. It is axiomatic and it is necessary and it is healthy. If another person is threatened by this, (they are to be minimized,) then it is they who are attempting to control and limit the spiritual journey of another. Such a selfish act. These people cannot possibly be on their own spiritual path if they must seek to censor and limit and control the path another is seeking.

ESSAY 87:
America, As an idea

America was founded as a promised land of new opportunities where people could escape their current circumstances and begin life anew in another far away location. It was a way to escape oppression and untenable conditions and start completely over in life. It was founded totally by immigration. Everyone came from "somewhere else". Thus, over the many years since its conception, it has become a test of sorts for "civilization" and the very survival of the human race.

How so, you may ask? America is different from every country in the world. All other countries are located in specific areas that were always occupied by similar races particular to that country. Asians had their own culture, customs, language, religion, physical attributes specific to their race, etc. Africans also. Scandinavians, Middle East, etc, etc. All these races existed eons before America was "founded".

So now we have a "modern" world that has become very small. Global travel makes it commonplace for all these cultures to become "threatened" by "outsiders" who are "different" from us. Due to politics, climate, economics, oppression, wars, etc, these countries are being inundated with people who look different, think differently, act differently from "us". Our very identity and culture is now under "attack". We are becoming something we no longer recognize or like. Who are we now, as a country?

America is the canary in the coal mine. This is so because America is totally about being the melting pot where people from every corner of the world can come and start a new life. America is so diverse with so many different cultures, belief systems, core values, etc. that what is happening with the American "experiment" portends the way the world will adapt, or not, to the rapidly changing realities of the 21st century. In America, people have to learn to be tolerant of those who are not "like us". We have to be able to adapt, to learn to work together as a people to solve the myriad of problems that are becoming a threat to the continuation of the human race. If the idea of America cannot resolve these present grave issues, there is no way the world can solve them. We will all be doomed.

As we can very readily see, America has a grade of "D" at best, in this test. We are more polarized, more prone to violence, more judgmental, less tolerant, and more rigid than ever in what we believe is the "right way" to do things. If America cannot come to common ground very soon, there is no way the world can make the necessary adjustments to be able to survive much longer. We have become so far removed from the original "promise" of learning to work together and reach a consensus of sorts, on the best way to solve our ever mounting problems.

I am of the opinion we have long since passed the tipping point on learning the crucial lessons that man must absorb to be able to insure the survival of the human race. My God, we cannot even agree on the best way to control a worldwide pandemic! If a pandemic does not, and it certainly has not, unite mankind in a fight for common survival of ourselves and loved ones, where do we go from here?! If that does not get everyone's attention, we are indeed lost. We must act immediately to change our ways. We are doing exactly the opposite! Get ready to pull the flush handle, for we are most assuredly circling the drain. I pray I am wrong about this.

ESSAY 88:

Gender, Sexuality, Authenticity, and Masks vs. Spiritual Truth

I am nearing 80 years of age as I compose this. I have been very fortunate throughout my life in many ways. One of the many gifts God granted me was a spiritual awareness at a fairly young age. In Junior High School and beyond, other students seemed to want to confide in me. They sensed something different, a sensitivity in me. Some tended to trust me with their secrets. They valued my opinions about their current circumstances. They knew I was safe. I never judged. The girls would feel secure in discussing their boy issues and vice versa.

Over the years, I have been privy to some private struggles that various friends have been dealing with. I have met and interacted with all kinds of people. Doing so has broadened and grown me. It has raised my awareness about many societal situations and issues. I have written before about different aspects of what I am about to discuss. Those essays set the stage for what follows.

When one is born, various feelings and desires and needs are assigned to us. Most are very basic. But many are unique to just us. What about a young male child who seems to be drawn to boys more than girls? Or girls who just seem to like girls more than boys? Why would anyone "choose" to have these "anti-normal" leanings? They are still too young to know the complications this will cause them by not being "normal". These are simply natural feelings they were born with. There is no right or wrong to the feelings of a child, so pure, unfiltered, honest.

Yet, when these children start to grow up and learn the "rules" of a "normal" society, the true test of their unique life begins. They may become confused and ask themselves questions. I feel this way but this way is "abnormal" so what is wrong with me? Nothing is wrong with you! You are just you! But society and its rules and expectations of you must be dealt with, sooner if possible. But for most, it is much later, if ever. I grew up in the 1940's, 50's and early 60's. Things have greatly improved since those dark ages, but much work still needs to be done. People are admitting who they are much sooner than in previous generations. More resources are available for help. Families are more accepting and supportive. The masks are being discarded much earlier.

I was divorced in the 1970's for a couple years. My barber was a very nice guy who became a friend who happened to be gay. He asked me one time if I would like to go to a nearby major city and meet some of his friends for a long weekend. I thought why not, this should be interesting. And was it ever! He took me to a gay bar that opened at 4pm on a Friday night. I had never been exposed to this environment and was curious as to what I may learn.

One of my first lasting impressions was to see all these professional men enter after 5 pm in their suits and ties. They all appeared successful and accomplished functioning in the "straight" world. The very first thing they did was to discard their suit coats, remove their ties and open their collars. They were ripping off their "straight" masks.! All the pretending was gone! You could instantly see and experience the transformation! Expressions of relief and pure joy replaced seriousness, They were greeting one another affectionately and enthusiastically. The feel was so different from so many straight bars. You could sense the honesty and connection among all of the patrons.

This bar also welcomed transvestites, ie. crossdressers, since these were men dressed as women. Some were gay, some not. I learned women had their lesbian bars too. They had no desire to be around men. Understandable. We visited one of those but were not welcome. The point is these individuals did not have to hide who they really are. In this setting, they were the normal ones! So liberating and necessary for them to be real, even for a short time, so they could embrace their power sources to better cope and function in their straight roles during the work week.

I visited this city a couple more times with my friend. On one visit, I met a Lakota Sioux Native American. He was not gay but we had something in common. I was familiar with his culture. We connected as friends. He told me he was going to transform into a woman. I had heard of this but never met a transexual before. In his culture, such individuals are considered gifted and special. As he shared this information with me, I thought "no way"! I just could not see it. He was very macho, masculine, burly and hairy, yet he had a sensitivity and tenderness about him. He told me he always knew he was different. His mother could see it in him. She told him he must be true to himself.

Of course, trying to fit in, he had lived the white man's life for over 30 years. He had his own construction company, served as a decorated helicopter pilot in the Vietnam War. But in his mid-30's he decided he could no longer stuff his deepest female feelings. He needed to be real, to himself and to God. I saw him after electrolysis and a year on female hormones. I could not believe the transformation! He was softer, not bulky, and was very stunning as a woman! He (she) was dating a woman who supported her 100% . She was so calm and serene and centered in her soon to be new life as a woman. She had figured it out much sooner than so many others such as she. One must be who he/she is to be real, before God, if one is to live an authentic life. To live authentically will lead you to great spiritual development. You become closer to God.

As I must state again, it is very difficult to have the courage to remove that protective mask. There are risks, but the rewards are eternal. It is safe in that "BOX". But a price is to be paid if one refuses to accept the feelings God granted you at your earliest awareness. These are feelings you did not request. But they are genuine. God is testing us. Do we follow His lead or do we live in denial for an entire lifetime? In denying ourselves at the core level, and we all know our true core, we are denying God, in my view.

This is such a sad and tragic way to live a singular life. But it is very understandable. I so respect and admire those who are "different" and yet grow to celebrate their being not like many others. They are putting all those feelings of shame and guilt behind them by undertaking this very difficult and sometimes dangerous, but very necessary action. To do this is a very courageous act that I believe God acknowledges and appreciates. It is also a quantum leap in spiritual growth in one lifetime. Life is just so full of tests, large and small, from our beginning to our end.

ESSAY 89:

My path

As previously stated, I am on my own spiritual path, as are we all, separate from my parents, their parents, my siblings, my aunts, uncles , cousins, my wife, my friends, my children, etc, etc, etc. As such, my earthly mission must be to focus on what I feel is correct for me to reach and honor my truth. The truth God instilled in me that I listen and pay close attention to every conscious moment of my life, at my deepest level. That voice that has been there for me since I was a small child. I started listening to it about age 9.

As I have been blessed to be able to fine tune my observations and conclusions, due to the fact I am still alive at 74+, I continue to reach my own conclusions. I am more patient with myself. I am at peace and most appreciative of this serenity arising from deep within. My entire life has been a process attempting to put forth maximum effort and getting my learnings. Where I am is where I am. I can live with that fact. I am well aware of the facts of my life and of the world, as much as I currently care to know about all these things, for I have zero control over any of it. I can attempt to control my reactions to these things and just keep going forward as best I can. Gotta let it go.

ESSAY 90:
Freedom of Choice and Fate of Mankind

God granted man freedom of choice, the ability to reason and make decisions. As a result, we are where we are today and we are accelerating to our demise. Think about it. Each individual human being is going to inherently act ultimately in his own best interest. He is wired to do so, and to survive he must, at a primal level, act in this manner.

Every person has his own reality, his own history, his own culture, his own DNA, his particular beliefs, his own interests, life experiences, and concepts about all sorts of things, and sees things from his own individual point of view for all types of reasons. Because of this, occasions will always arise when his best interests will be in conflict with those of another person. So, potential conflict is inevitable in any given interaction with another person. The problem today is that conflicts are everywhere we look all over the world. They exist between individuals, at work and at home, in communities, in business, government, and among nations.

These differences of opinion are destroying societies. Those in power are suppressing and oppressing the weaker. Increasing exploitation and domination are rampant worldwide. We have created a have and have-not divide that is quantum, and growing rather than diminishing. The lessers of the world have reached the point where they feel they have nothing to lose by standing up for the few crumbs they are allowed to have. They want more and they are increasingly taking action to get it. But in doing so, conflict cannot be prevented. And the costs to those in power are too great to allow this to happen. The powerful are reaching for more and more and when one constantly wants "more", there is never "enough". So we will always fight one another until we have destroyed the human race and much of the world as we know it today. I see this as the end point of man and I can see no way it can be avoided.

It is so obvious that some current political "leaders" are greatly accelerating this divide. BTW, General Custer considered himself and perhaps some others did also, a "great leader"! Not a happy ending! But other governments are also doing similar things in controlling their populations that will tend to grow to outright rebellion. Exhibit A is in Syria and the result is a completely destroyed nation. So it will be with the entire planet. Civilization will be destroyed to "save" it for the powers that be. They "won"!!??

More developed or evolved human beings see the wisdom and dire necessity for cooperation and compromise and all the mutual benefits this can offer mankind by doing so. They try to resolve conflicts early on for the benefit of the whole. To be violent is not in their nature. They try to avoid these primitive inclinations because they know where this leads. However, the powerful see this as passiveness, a weakness to be exploited. They are very prone to use all methods possible to enact their personal agendas. These individuals are not evolved human beings and they are very successful in suppressing and silencing the more spiritual ones among our species.

We, as humans, have so many means now available to initiate and perpetuate our own demise. Each of these could become flash points or allow us to reach the kindling temperature required to "set ourselves on fire" and destroy ourselves. Take your pick. Artificial intelligence.

More "sophisticated" weapons systems. DNA manipulation and modification, ie. genetic engineering of human beings. Overpopulation and dwindling natural resources to support the populations. Lessened effectiveness of antibiotics and more likely the possibility of a world-wide pandemic. Fiat money and world-wide economic collapse and depression. Severe and most likely irreversible catastrophic climate change.

The problem has become that rather than becoming more united as a species, we are more divided than ever and a divided entity cannot survive. Only harmonious systems in the universe survive. Human beings are not harmonious. This is a very evident fact to anyone who pays attention.

But we have arrived, or even surpassed our tipping point on this planet. We are accelerating to our fate. This is very sad to admit and very pessimistic of course, but from my perspective looking down from way above, it is so very obvious. And it is now as it must be. We have sown these seeds all by ourselves and we are now beginning to pay the price. God has nothing to do with this. He granted us freedom to choose and this is what we have chosen. Soon enough will come the reckoning.

The universes continue to grow and expand and thrive and mankind is but a miniscule, very brief blip in the grand scheme. We are nothing. Much, much, much more spiritual, sophisticated, developed and evolved life forms inhabit other worlds all thru the vastness of uncountable galaxies. Of this, I have absolute, total and complete certainty and profound faith. The human race is too flawed to last the long haul. It will "extinct" itself without any help from an incoming errant asteroid or meteor collision, thank you.

ESSAY 91:

Lord's Prayer... My Interpretation

I believe the Lord's Prayer to be the most profound and elegant composition of prose even written. It is concise, clear, simple, yet deep. It truly speaks to those who are listening. By listen, I refer to deeply thinking about every word or phrase and absorbing it to the very core of your being. I personally recite this to myself almost daily, sometimes more than once, when the time seems right. There is a right time-always. It relaxes me. It puts me in my moment. It centers me and gives me a peaceful mind and provides a safe secure sanctuary from which I can function more efficiently throughout my day.

By really concentrating on what I am reciting to myself, I am acutely aware of God being with me at that very moment and actively in my life. It takes me deeper within myself so it becomes more familiar and easier for me to get to my inner spirit, that place from which all my answers come. My spirit is what guides me, for God gifted me my soul and by making it habitual to gain this deep access from within myself, I am in direct communication with God on a regular basis. Again, this is spiritual, not religious per se. This connection is so beyond the boundaries of religious doctrine. It is so much deeper, for me.

Following is what these precious words mean to me. My interpretation..

"Our Father"...He is not just my Father, He is the Father of all that was, is, and shall ever be. He is OUR Father. That brings me a sense of connection to the ONE, the everything. I am nothing special personally but yet I am special. As are we all special in God's eyes. That sense of connection to Father makes me feel safe, secure, taken care of, and loved unconditionally. That lets me know He has my back, no matter what. No conditions, no judgement, no blame or condemnation, no rejection, no abandonment issues. With His love and support, my life is full of opportunities to grow, develop, reach my full potential, to soar in life, IF I take action.

"who art in Heaven"...Heaven is where God 'lives' we may think. But God is everywhere, so He is on Earth also. So Heaven exists on Earth. Heaven exists within all of us, again, IF we pay attention. Heaven is not a "place" in itself. It can be a state of mind, a consciousness. It is not an end point, nor a destination point. When God is in Heaven, He is also within all of us. That being said, I do believe that Heaven exists. There has to be a much better place awaiting all of us at the end of our physical life. But again God is there.

"hallowed be thy name" ...Such a beautiful phrase! Hold Him in awe with gratitude and utmost respect. His name is be held in honor and with supreme reverence. His name is sacred. Etched in our minds and souls forever.

"thy kingdom come" ... We will join Him soon enough. We are invited to join Him and are most welcome there. Our "seat" is reserved, forever. No lines, no doubts. No uncertainty exists.

"thy will be done"...He will decide when we shall come home again. He has all the power, we have none that matters. His will is also present in all our actions and reactions. He will decide what path our life will take. What hardships must we encounter, what losses, what victories? However, we are responsible for the choices we make in life. These choices we make do have consequences and we will be held accountable, in some manner. But at our end, it is God who decides our fate.

"on Earth as it is in Heaven"… Again, Earth and Heaven are the same in that God is with us always. It is a continuum and there is no separation. There is only connection. And that gives me serenity. I am part of all that is.

"Give us Lord our daily bread"… Allow us to be able to meet our most basic needs of food, water, and shelter on a daily basis so we may survive another day. It does NOT mean to take all you can! It does NOT mean to accumulate more than you require at the expense of the needs of others. It means to just be able to provide what you need, not what you want!

"and forgive us our trespasses as we forgive those who trespass against us"…Forgive us for actions we have taken, intentionally or not, that did harm to others. We want to grow to recognize our bad behaviors and strive to become better people by eliminating these incidents. ….We must try to forgive those who do us wrong. By forgiving them, we are regaining our power for we move on and let it go. By dismissing it we remove it from within us. However, we must use this betrayal as a learning opportunity. We will become wiser and know more about that person. Thus, we will be more cautious and we will not forget. Not to get even, for that still means that transgressors still have power over you.

"Lead us not into temptation"… Do not get yourself into situations that may result in potential harm. This could be economic harm, substance harm, marriage harm, self-harm, etc. When you are tempted to do a certain act, something is enticing you. Something is seducing you. Your hesitation is a sign of caution to proceed carefully, if you proceed at all. So, you know that uncertainty and danger and consequences may await. So God is just stating to be careful. Be hesitant. Listen to your internal voice. And be willing to address the consequences of your decision.

"and deliver us from evil"... Protect and allow us to move beyond terrible actions done by others that affect our lives. We must gain the strength to overcome these events and become stronger having suffered greatly and move forward with our lives. Having endured evil and survived will have made us stronger spiritually, at some point in time.

"For thine is the kingdom, the power, and the glory forever, AMEN." Thine is all that is. And that says it all. So elegantly stated. A perfect conclusion that is a true forever statement of Divine and eternal truth. There is absolutely no room for any doubt in this profound sentence. We all know who the "boss" is and we rejoice in this bedrock conviction of its absolute veracity.

When you communicate on a regular basis with God via the Lord's Prayer, you will come to recognize He is also communicating with you. You will become more familiar and comfortable with each other. You will find you have less need for ego and you will become humbled.

ESSAY 92:
In Summation...My gift? ... One Hundredth Monkey Effect

As I have mentioned before, I had a very dear, intelligent and talented friend who passed away two years ago after a brief illness of brain cancer. He was truly a Renaissance Man, so beloved by many and very gifted! As we both were well aware his remaining days were very short, it was time for total honesty.I shared some of my essays with him. He told me how valuable they were and commented that I had a "great mind" and should continue writing and to share it with the masses. I disagree with him on one point. I believe I do have an adequate mind, but I certainly do not consider myself a great intellect. However, I am a very deep spiritual thinker and I am well aware and very comfortable with my relationship with my Maker. I attempt to put my beliefs into words that many will hopefully be able to understand, on some level.

My goal for this book has been to share my thoughts, insights, and truths with the reader with the objective of their being better equipped and prepared to navigate through all the trials and tribulations of life. I wish for us all to arrive at a place of PEACE, within ourselves, of ALL that IS. The human condition is such that the only true serenity must come from the internal, for the external will never achieve a peaceful place. It is thus a challenge for each individual to get to this precious place, deep within, for that is the only space that is truly safe. It is also the only way one can hope to make some sense of all the inequities and true absurdities that always have and shall continue to exist in living externally.

My most ambitious wish is that enough people can reach "critical mass" in their spiritual journeys so that the "One Hundredth Monkey Effect" type of awareness can be achieved globally. According to Wikipedia, this is a hypothetical phenomenon in which a new behavior or idea is spread rapidly from one group to all related groups once a critical number of members of one group exhibit the new behavior or acknowledge the new idea. How humble is that!? I feel without this global transformation we will soon enough extinct ourselves.

So please take your time. Read these essays and axioms. Read them many times. Take pause, examine them, ponder them, challenge them, re-visit them as needed. Draw your strength from them by striving to get more in touch with the divinity within you, and allow your spirit, your soul to guide you by being intimately in touch with Him. He will show you the way forward, when you learn to truly pay attention and listen, from deep within. Share these words with dear people special to you in their times of duress or need for guidance. We just must strive to help one another in any way we can. The best way to do this is to help yourself become centered and whole and then use your God-given strength and power to aid others who need the gifts of wisdom and connection you have gained for yourself. We indeed are all ONE, truly blessed by God. Be at peace....Amen.

ESSAY 93:

AXIOMS... Observations and Truisms for Guidance in Life Lessons

1. Always put forth a good effort.

2. Use your time wisely.

3. Work and live with passion.

4. Believe and invest in yourself.

5. Love.

6. Expect change.

7. Adapt to change.

8. Do not surrender your power.

9. Have a vision.

10. Be empathic.

11. Visit foreign countries.

12. Contribute.

13. Discover your purpose.

14. Everything is temporary.

15. Reframe a challenge into an opportunity.

16 Do not be a critic unless prepared to offer a solution.

17. Pull the trigger.

18. Ask questions.

19. Figure it out on your own.

20. Accept consequences of your decisions.

21. Do not judge.

22. Accept a set-back as temporary and an opportunity for growth.

23. Listen first, speak second.

24. Accept responsibility.

25. Do not condemn.

26. Read

27. Cultivate friendships.

28. Expect loss.

27. Travel.

28. Help somebody.

29. Be physically and mentally active.

30. Make commitments and keep them.

31. ID your power sources.

32. Keep learning.

33. Take calculated risks.

34. Share.

35. Live honorably.

36. Be a mentor.

37. Do something bigger than yourself.

38. Pain will end.

39. Keep your word.

40. Make a difference.

41. Create time for yourself.

42. Do not fear failure.

43. Create memories.

44. Set up a tent in your backyard for your children..

45. Understand suffering.

46. Give back.

47. Eat healthy.

48. Smile often.

49. Appreciate that life is a wondrous gift, no matter what.

50. Take a stand.

51. Listen to your body, and pay attention.

52. Reward yourself, from time to time.

53. Have an opinion.

54. Examine what is between the lines.

55. Be a reluctant follower.

56. Do your homework.

57. Trust must be earned.

58. Mistakes are great teachers.

59. Learn something every single day.

60. Ask for help.

61. Be patient.

62. Material things don't last.

63. Sometimes you need to just tread water.

64. Answers come from within.

65. Be willing to pay a price.

66. Never compromise your values.

67. Obey God's Laws over man's laws.

68. Take regular vacations.

69. Know when to take a step back.

70. Know the difference between want and need.

71. Break up your routines.

72. Be reliable.

73. Get sufficient rest.

74. In the end, you truly are alone.

75. Observe and experience sunrises and sunsets.

76. Say I am sorry.

77. Do not allow someday to become yesterday, live today.

78. Create and appreciate periods of solitude.

79. It is up to you.

80. Recognize that what you have is enough.

81. Be moral.

82. Security comes from within.

83. Keep it simple.

84. Be humble.

85. Minimize noise and clutter.

86. Write thank you notes.

87. Be gracious.

88. Know you are blessed.

89. It is not about you.

90. Sometimes, you have to fight.

91. ID and honor the flow of all things.

92. Get regular massages.

93. Speak your mind.

94. Serenity comes from within.

95. Talk to God.

96. Pay attention to your surroundings.

97. Wipe your own butt.

98. Be aware.

99. Keep in touch.

100. Observe and appreciate nature.

101. Be a forever student.

102. Get outdoors in the sun.

103. Control is an illusion.

104. You are your own security.

105. Spend time in/on/near the water.

106. Smell the flowers.

107. Walk barefoot in wet grass.

108. Roll in a pile of fresh fallen autumn leaves with your children.

109. Have a plan, etched in sand.

110. Be proactive, rather than reactive.

111. Speak with your actions.

112. Say thank you.

113. What if the life you are living is the dream and Heaven is the reality?

114. Make snow angels.

115. Walk barefoot on the beach.

116. You will never be lonely if you are comfortable with the person you are alone with.

117. Skinny dip.

118. Go fishing.

119. Hunt with a camera, not a gun.

120. Climb mountains.

121. Kayak mountain lakes at sunrise and sunset.

122. Observe and listen to wildlife and birds. They are great teachers!

123. Go skiing after a fresh snowfall.

124. Teach your children to play chess.

125. Teach your children to play and love sports.

126. Play in team sports, great lessons for life.

127. Provide a welcoming and safe haven for your children to have their friends over.

128. Help with coaching your children's team sports.

129. Learn to play an individual sport that you can play for a lifetime, for it keeps you active and provides an avenue to cultivate great and lasting friendships.

130. Set an example.

131. Never be perceived as a snob.

132. You are not better than anyone. You are different.

133. Aspire to the developmental level where you truly can appreciate that giving TO someone is so much more gratifying than taking FROM them.

134. After meeting one's basic needs, it is never about the money.

135. Never look down on anybody. They have attributes too.

136. Do not be a whiner or complainer.   Take action.

137. It is not "someone else's fault." It is what it is. Deal with it!

138. If you must burn a bridge to take a stand, burn the damned bridge!

139. Do not throw away what you no longer need. Give it away.

140. Try to first learn to fix things, rather than simply junk them.

141. Strive to live a truly examined life.

142. Do not ever be fearful of testing yourself.

143. Be cautiously prepared, rather than fearful.

144. Uncertainty and doubt is minimized by careful preparation in advance of the event.

145. Biographies are wonderful teachers of examples of lives lived, warts and all.

146. Do not hesitate to spend a little more extra money if it will provide you an unique opportunity to create a memory to last a lifetime. You will forget the money soon enough, but will always cherish and savor that very precious, irreplaceable, and forever memory!

147. Money is the means, NEVER the end!

148. Reach out to those in need and do so with ZERO expectations.

149. People and loved ones will disappoint you. Have no expectations on your part. Do NOT take it personally! They are where they are and you are where you are. They have their journey and you have yours. Honor where they are. So be it.

150. Never harbor a grudge. Doing so is to surrender your power to another who can never take your power from you UNLESS you permit him to do so!

151. Do not envy anyone, ever! Your very own divinely endowed, and personal and special God-given gift of life is uniquely yours alone. Honor your very special treasure till the end!

152. Do not be attached to outcomes. Deal with it.

153. Respect genius and passion in others.

154. Defer to no one.

155. Never willingly give in.

156. Nothing is as it first appears.   Dig deeper.

157. Most everyone has an agenda.

158. Never betray a trust.

159. Try not to gossip.

160. Once trust is lost, it can never be fully regained.

161. What is "legal" is not always moral.

162. Be a mediator.

163. A person who cheats will always cheat.

164. Do not obey all the rules just because they are 'rules".

165. Dare to be unique.

166. Seek the company of positive people.

167. Trust in yourself.

168. Pay attention to your conscience.

169. Be careful how you state things.

170. Learn to play a musical instrument.

171. Live your life as a long distance event, not as a sprint.

172. Do it the right way, but be willing to "round it off" at appropriate times.

173. Be flexible.

174. Be cautiously optimistic when applicable, but not naively so.

175. If you truly feel it, be enthusiastic!

176. Sometimes you just must let go.

177. Do not be afraid to embarrass yourself at times.

178. Give great tight lingering hugs!

179. Challenge yourself.

180. Do not be an enabler to weaker people.

181. Exhibit self-love rather than selfish love and know the important difference.

182. Touch people by your words AND your actions.

183. Do the right thing.

184. Take the time to really listen to rain on a metal roof.

185. Enjoy a guilt-free ice cream cone from time to time, not a dish.

186. Men, grow a beard at least once. Women, grow your hair long sometimes.

187. Allow your kids the complete freedom to pick out and dress themselves, when appropriate.

188. Do not attempt to control all aspects of your children's lives. Allow them to make decisions and learn from them.

189. Do not "suffocate" your children with "love". They are meant to grow up and leave the nest.

190. Men, always have one good suit available to wear.

191. Always be groomed well enough in public.

192. Brush your teeth after breakfast and floss and brush before bedtime!

193. Try to watch your weight but do not obsess about it.

194. Do not manipulate people with guilt.

195. Do not use people for personal gain.

196. It is necessary to ask your employer for a deserved raise. If you do not believe you deserve it, neither will your boss.

197. When interviewing for a new job, educate yourself about the position and inform the interviewer what you have to offer the company, rather than ask what does the company have to offer you.

198. Be a team player.

199. If no one takes the lead, if necessary, step up and do it. Do not be afraid to lead. It gets easier.

200. You can only be used by another person with your permission.

201. Be a dreamer.

202. Take your family camping.

203. You do not need "permission" from anyone to live your life.

204. Do not live your life seeking or needing "approval" from anyone, except yourself.

205. Do not "expect" anything, but you can certainly hope and work for it.

206. The "government" will not save you.

207. There is no pot of gold or fairy princess or Prince Charming.

208. Keep the "child" alive in you, always.

209. It is OK to "request" someone change their behavior but understand they may be unable or unwilling to do so.

210. Do not back down from a just cause.

211. Do not take "hope" away from another person.

212. Remove yourself from negative people and negative situations.

213. There is always another way.

214. To make peace, you sometimes must apologize even when you are right. Take the higher road.

215. No one wins an argument. Let the other party state their case and you state yours. Then refuse to discuss it further till the other person calms down. Be prepared to wait days, or longer.

216. Kill your opponent with kindness initially. This will soften them up. They will lower their guard so then you can make your point obliquely, but clearly.

217. When you directly verbally attack a person, you place them on the defensive. Thus, they will defend and attack you back. True communication then becomes impossible, for no one is listening. Best to use the above approaches (#215-216) for a more desired outcome.

218. Demonstrate a genuine interest in other people and they will reciprocate.

219. Never criticize another person in public or in front of co-workers. Do it one-on-one in private.

220. Be generous with compliments and praise of others and their actions.

221. Do not hog another person's glory.

222. Never interrupt another person while they are speaking. Allow them to finish.

223. Not wise to add your two cents unless it is requested. The recipient will resent it and surely will reject it.

224. You are not an expert in everything, actually not in anything.

225. When speaking to another person and their eyes "glaze over" or they start looking away, redirect the topic directly to them, or exit the conservation before they do. Actually, they already have.

226. Do not "insinuate yourself" into a conservation that people are actively engaged in. You ruin their flow and it is rude, selfish, unsolicited, and resented.

227. Be present.

228. Deliver more than you promise.

229. Choose healthy escapes, not chemical ones.

230. Attend live theater when you can.

231. Support children's lemonade stands.

232. Bake homemade cookies from time to time.

233. Make savings a habit, but not an end in itself.

234. Learn to make simple repairs.

235. Live beneath your means.

236. Don't crap in your own nest.

237. Appreciate beauty wherever it exists.

238. Teach your children to iron and cook.

239. Support local merchants frequently.

249. Health is more important than wealth.

250. Respect and appreciate differences.

251. Go on a hot air balloon ride.

252. Better to be underestimated than to be overestimated.

253. Diversify.

254. Because I am "right" does not have to mean you are "wrong". People have different realities.

255. There truly is a reason for everything, but sometimes we will never know. Gotta go deeper and look higher.

256. Try to avoid making others feel they are "less than"....

257. Stand up for your rights.

258. Try to maintain a longer fuse, rather than a short one.

259. Dissent, when appropriate.

260. Offer your adversary an honorable way out.

261. Allow your partner to be an individual, not a reflection or extension of you.

262. Fly under the radar.

263. Drink champagne once in a while.

264. Make yourself proud but do not wear that fact on your sleeve.

265. Enjoy fine dining when given the opportunity.

266. Risk being silly on occasion.

267. Always desiring more can be a destroyer of life.

268. Celebrate your victories.

270. Take calculated risks, not careless ones.

271. Appearance matters.

272. Halos do not fit well on swelled heads.

273. Take frequent pictures of occasions and scenes that move you.

274. Keep a journal. It becomes a safe place to examine and process your thoughts.

275. Take good care of your back and your feet. Do not skimp on a bed or proper shoes.

276. You have the right to say NO.

277. Laugh a lot.

276. If you have serious doubts, back off and let it simmer.

277. Experience an authentic "endorphin high" at least once in your life.

278. Something you truly earn has much more value than that which is simply given to you.

279. What you think of me is not my business, it is yours.

280. Never trust a social climber.

281. A person who talks about others to you, will talk about you to others.

282. Try to avoid killing any animal ever. Seek to relocate the nuisance ones.

283. If safely possible, remove exposed turtles from the open highway.

284. Marvel at the energy of the sun. Look towards it with your eyes closed and truly absorb it! How do you feel?!

285. Be careful what you say in anger.

286. Believe in GOD completely, but the action part is totally up to you.

287. Many people seek and want approval, but secure people do not need it.

288. Takers will always take.

289. The majority is often wrong. Group think.

290. Be kind to animals and insects too.

291. Do not be ashamed or reluctant to cry.

292. Choose to live your life in the arena, not on the sidelines.

293. Working at a meaningful job truly feeds the soul, and It is a necessity.

294. Step lightly, but wear heavy soled shoes.

295. Aim for excellence, rather than perfection.

296. Give a damn.

297. Know your limits, but do not be afraid to push and expand them.

298. Display kind eyes.

299. Seek the simplest solution first.

300. Be pragmatic.

301. We are all spiritual beings living a physical life. Too many have no awareness.

302. Do not just say you care, show you care.

303. Become disciplined.

304. Evolve.

305. Nothing positive results from staying out past midnight.

306. Try to take a major trip once a year. It grows you and it is necessary.

307. Be tolerant with inconvenience.

308. When exhausted, do one more lap.

309. Know when it is time to blow out the candle.

310. Sometimes, a person just needs to be held.

311. Be benevolent.

312. Avoid firing anyone. Rather, offer them the opportunity to find employment elsewhere that better suits their gifts and talents.

313. Remember, you can almost always make more money, but you cannot make more time.

314. If you "always" want more, you will "never" have enough.

315. It is important to own your own home at some point in your life. There is great satisfaction derived from working together to maintain it and make it better.

316. Grant yourself permission to succeed.

317. Highly spiritual people tend to be more mentally and morally strong and centered.

318. Spiritual individuals just seem to "know" and others tend to sense this about them.

319. Never be afraid to change the way you think.

320. Government never controls itself. It seeks to control the people.

321. Takers will always take.

322. The majority is often wrong. Group think is easier.

323. Believe in a higher power and trust in Him, but the ACTION part is up to you.

324. To an honorable person, truth is more important than the perception of truth held by others.

325. What you believe about me is not my concern. It is yours.

326. Many people seek and desire approval, but secure people do not need it. However, it does feel nice when you get it.

327. Recognize, acknowledge, and be cognizant that "your" life is only "loaned" to you.

328. People who always have an excuse, will always have an excuse. You cannot depend on them.

329. You will need at some points, to retain your integrity, directly confront a person or a situation.

330. Do not be reluctant to go out of your way to aid someone you care about to become all that they can be. You CAN make a difference, but to do so you must make a sincere, focused, and dedicated effort.

331. Living more simply will lead to living more peacefully and happily.

332. Never permit yourself to be painted into a corner. You surrender your power. Be prepared and be careful.

333. Be smart and anticipatory and plan forward. Always create and reserve enough space to be able to maneuver in different directions in any negotiation or life circumstance.

334. Learn to not be impulsive. Wait 24 hours (+) before making any major purchase or decision. Sleep on it. Ruminate.

335. Be patient enough to learn to recognize and observe the flow of life. Swim with the current, not against it. All the answers eventually become evident to the keen and astute observer.

336. Listen! ... Observe! ... Process! ... Act! "LOPA". (JHW acronym)

337. Do not be afraid of fear. Fear is a primal early warning system. Rather, take a pause, evaluate, then decide any possible course of action needed and proceed with appropriate caution and care.

338. Work at something, in some capacity, that you truly enjoy for as many years as you can. It gives your life purpose, meaning, stimulation, monetary rewards, balance, and social interaction. All these things are very necessary to stay actively involved as you travel the path of life.

339. Users will always use.

340. Take your time and learn to enjoy and appreciate the journey, for the destination will frequently change.

341. Too much comfort/security can tend to impede your personal growth.

342. Having much more money or possessions than you really need can be crippling in that you tend to spend too much valuable time and energy in keeping them, protecting them, or growing them.

343. Helping somebody "could" be considered a selfish act, for it makes YOU feel good! So, that is a positive "selfish", if it is even selfish at all.

344. Be a contributor.

345. We are all on a continuum.

346. Strive to make the most of a negative situation. Put your head down and work through it.

347. Aim to achieve peace of mind in all that you do.

348. Forgive your flaws. Work on them, learn from them and move on.

349. Prepare yourself for a possible negative outcome, but make every effort to achieve a positive one. This helps you better deal with set-backs.

350. When speaking to someone, look them directly in the eye. That conveys interest and strength.

351. When presented with a "honey do" list by your mate or someone else, if not convenient to you, establish some boundaries. Do it more on your schedule, rather than theirs.

352. Appreciate your past, but do not live there.

353. Show up.

354. When you feel strongly you are right, stand your ground.

355. You may, at times, find it wise to surrender a position. Then regroup to gain an advantage.

356. As in sailing, sometimes you may need to make a tac to get where you want to go.

357. Have a valid passport.

358. Learn to change a tire.

359. Know CPR and basic first aid.

360. Observe ant colonies and bee hives. "Socialism" at work??

361. Vote.

362. Do not hike in the wild alone.

363. Take a walk regularly.

364. Know how to swim and teach your children.

365. Ride a bike from time to time.

366. Try to have enough cash, not in a bank, to cover three months' expenses. Fifties and twenties.

367. Have some hobbies or activities you really are passionate about.

368. Develop a sense of humor.

369. Seek balance in life.

370. When appropriate, question, and when necessary, challenge authority.

371. If need be, dissent. Defend your position and try to offer another solution.

372. Blaze your own trail.

373. To go along to get along does not grow you. It is easier. Do not live your life this way, but it may prove necessary at times.

374. Prepare yourself for the worse, but plan for the best.

375. While one should be most appreciative of the gift of life as a human being, also recognize that life as it is typically lived in modern society, is mostly BS.

376. You are not more or less than someone else, you are different than.

377. Get a dog, or have a pet.

378. You make more money with your brain than with your back. And your brain grows stronger as your back becomes weaker.

379. We all have our unique God given gifts. Discover yours and develop them.

380. Coahulla Nation: Real Eyes. Realize. Real Lies.

Keywords for Kindle searching:

Spirituality; Soul; Existential; Truisms, Divinity; Eternity; Awareness

General Information about the book "Teaser"

This book was intended to be a series of essays and axioms about my beliefs of life to pass on to my children. I wanted a primer for them to refer to when they may seek some guidance after I have passed on. My hope is for the reader to learn how to live more in the spirit world, the only world that truly matters.These reflect my conclusions about human nature, the current human condition and spirituality. They are a result of observations and personal interactions with thousands of people over my lifetime. These are strong opinions, truisms and guidelines for life that have percolated from deep within me, for multiple decades. We are all on this brief visit of life together. Let us each attempt to make an effort to ease the burdens of others. This in one of my contributions.

About Author:

He is highly educated, has a doctorate degree and has been writing his entire life. He realized very early that he had sensitivities and insights that many others did not appear to have. He could sense and perceive things. This book is a culmination of his conclusions gleaned from a lifetime approaching eighty years.

Thank you for reading!

I realize there is some deep material on many subjects. I hope you gained some value from this book and found it provoking or useful. I would be very grateful if you would post a brief review on Amazon.

I read all reviews and your input is useful to me. I appreciate it! Onward!

Dr. Jac.
www.infinitymanspirit.com.
Email..infinitymanspirit@gmail.com